CHILDREN OF PROMISE

CHILDREN OF PROMISE

THE LAMANITES: YESTERDAY & TODAY

Mark E. Petersen

Bookcraft
Salt Lake City, Utah

Library of Congress Catalog Card Number: 81-67310
ISBN O-88494-431-X

First Printing, 1981

Lithographed in the United States of America
PUBLISHERS PRESS
Salt Lake City, Utah

CONTENTS

PART I   A PEOPLE OF PROPHECY

1 A Miracle of Miracles   5
2 The Divine Promise   8
3 The Lamanite Missions............................ 11
4 Their Greatest Mission 14
5 The Appeal at Cumorah 17

PART II   THE GREAT DISPERSION

6 The Trail of Tears 25
7 They Go Their Ways 31
8 The Maya and the Inca 36
9 The Olmecs and the Aztecs...................... 39
10 Polynesians and Mound Builders 41
11 Ancient Visitors 44

PART III   THE LORD KEEPS HIS WORD

12 The "Nursing Fathers" 51
13 Indian Government 54
14 What BYU Does 56
15 The Gospel Comes 59
16 The Gospel to the Lamanites 63
17 The Mission Begins 66
18 South Seas Missions 71
19 The Hawaiian Mission 73
20 Presidents Smith and McKay 79
21 Matthew Cowley's Saga 81
22 The Work Increases 84
23 Church Opportunities 87

PART I

A PEOPLE
OF PROPHECY

THE LAMANITES
Charles W. Penrose

Ye Indian tribes, who roam in
    countless bands
From north to south in yonder
    western lands,
With fiery, flashing eye and stately
    tread,
With tawny skin and proudly lifted
    head,
Whose lusty yell affrights the
    shivering air
And drives the timid settler to
    despair.
Why do ye restless wander thus
    abroad?
Why is your darkened skin of this
    red hue?
What is your origin? From whence
    are you?

A MIRACLE
OF MIRACLES

One of the greatest miracles of all time is unfolding before us, bringing joy and rejoicing to many, although leaving some incredulous.

But there it is, in all its glory, literally revealing the Almighty walking in His majesty. It is one of the most convincing of the signs of the times.

And what is it? It is the restitution of the Lamanites to their proper place in the kingdom of God. The promises of old are being fulfilled, and the descendants of Lehi indeed begin to blossom as the rose.

It is a missionary story, an epoch of conversion to rank with anything in gospel history. Lamanites were brought into the Church anciently and received of its blessings, but today they come to Christ by the hundreds of thousands as "fellow citizens with the Saints and of the household of God."

The Lamanites are a western hemisphere people. They have been since the days of Lehi and still are. But they also stretch out to the distant islands of the seas.

At no time did the Lord ever "give up" on the Lamanites. They were always children of promise. He is now fulfilling those promises as these descendants of Lehi and Joseph, Abraham, Isaac and Jacob, begin to see the light of Christ. They have had a colorful life, filled with tragedies and complexities, but now they begin to come into the place which God designed for them.

Through the centuries the Lamanites have experienced widely differing modes of life. Some developed the pueblo culture of the Southwest. Others formed great tribal confederations like the Iroquois in the Northeast.

Millions became Incas, Zapotecs, Olmecs, Toltecs, Aztecs and Mayans and achieved a civilization equal to that of the Europeans of the same time period.

Many drifted over the wide Pacific and set up a culture distinctly their own in the warm Polynesian Islands.

Columbus found Indians when he reached American shores. So did the Pilgrims. Captain John Smith met them at Jamestown.

On the western plains they engaged United States' troops in bitter wars to save their homes and hunting grounds as encroaching wagon trains moved toward the setting sun.

Battles like Custer's Last Stand became repetitive. Settlers' homes and farms in America were burned by raiders who made capital of every scalp they took, only to suffer equally severe retaliation from the "paleface" whom they sought to restrain.

Peace came to them in America, but only by the sword — the white man's sword — when the Indians were defeated on all fronts and were driven onto reservation lands which were considered of no value yet quite good enough for the Indians. There these unfortunate peoples were virtually imprisoned although their only offense was that they had fought for survival, for their homes and livelihood. Thus they were brought down to the dust. In other lands they fought among themselves, finally falling prey to cruel invaders.

But the prophets said that great changes would come in this latter day, two kinds of changes. One would be that governments which defeated them would become their nursing fathers and mothers. This has had a dramatic fulfillment in some nations.

The other change would bring the light of the gospel to lead them back to the kingdom of God. This heavenly action would include an ancient record, a book destined to come out of the ground, a history of their ancestors. It would tell them whence they came and whither they may yet go.

The record "was written to the Lamanites who are a remnant of the House of Israel" and came also "by way of commandment and by the Spirit of prophecy and of revelation — written and sealed up and hid up unto the Lord" to come forth in "due time by way of the Gentile." (Frontispiece of the Book of Mormon.)

This great modern miracle does come "by way of the Gentile" through the labors of the Prophet Joseph Smith and the missionary work he introduced among the Lamanites. He personally labored among them.

6

This missionary endeavor now has expanded internationally and opens to the family of Lehi a vast door to the future. A portal now beckons them even to take part in preparations for the second coming of Christ!

What a transition! What an opportunity for a people so long veiled in darkness!

The day of the Lamanite in very truth is the day of Christ! It looks toward a millennium of peace. The righteous among them will accept the Savior—multitudes already have—and their descendants may yet live to reign with the King of kings for a thousand years.

THE DIVINE
PROMISE

Tremendous conflict between the people of the United States and the descendants of Laman and Lemuel was clearly predicted in scripture, and the prophecies were fulfilled to the letter.

Two thousand years before there was a "gentile nation" on this land, the prophet Nephi saw in vision that the "seed of my brethren" would be driven, scattered, and trodden down by the colonists of America.

He said, "I beheld the wrath of God that it was upon the seed of my brethren and they were scattered before the Gentiles and smitten." (1 Nephi 13:14.) But he also saw brighter days.

The Indians, of course, were the possessors of the western hemisphere for centuries before the Europeans came. America was their home. It was all they knew and loved.

When the "Gentiles" began their settlements in America and moved west from one coast to the other, the Indians regarded them as interlopers who were robbing them of the lands they had roamed so freely for generations.

To flee before them meant surrender of all they possessed. They determined to fight in defense of their homelands, as many other peoples have done, indeed as the American settlers themselves did when the British and the French rose against them.

They also fought like their brethren southward in Mexico and those in South America who opposed intrusions there. Were they not justified in their war of self-defense?

They did not regard themselves as aggressors in any sense. They were defenders of their families, homes, hunting grounds—their all. And when they attacked the white set-

8

tlers they did so in the same spirit in which white soldiers fought to preserve their own homes in other battles.

Home is home to all peoples, and all peoples have an inherent spirit of self-defense. This the Indians also had, and they exercised it. But although they won some battles, eventually they were defeated on all fronts and brought down to humiliation and confinement.

However, Nephi's vision given six hundred years before Christ and long before there were any Lamanites or American colonists, offered assurance of hope for their ultimate survival and development.

As Nephi's view of the future unfolded, an angel of God stood by him and said: "The Lord will not suffer that the Gentiles will utterly destroy the mixture of thy seed which are among thy brethren, neither will he suffer that the Gentiles shall destroy the seed of thy brethren."

But the Lord did not stop there. He pledged to preserve this family—now in the millions of population—that a remnant of them in turn would receive the light of the gospel and join with their brethren, the modern families of Ephraim, in establishing the kingdom of God on earth preparatory to the second coming of Christ.

"There are many promises which are extended to the Lamanites, for it is because of the traditions of their fathers that caused them to remain in their state of ignorance. Therefore the Lord will be merciful unto them and prolong their existence in the land.

"And at some period of time they will be brought to believe in his word and to know of the incorrectness of the traditions of their fathers, and many of them will be saved, for the Lord will be merciful unto all who call on his name." (Alma 9:16-17.)

This is another most interesting prophecy:

"The Lord will raise up a mighty nation among the Gentiles, yea, even upon the face of this land, and by them shall our seed be scattered.

"And after our seed is scattered, the Lord will proceed to do a marvelous work among the Gentiles, which shall be of great worth unto our seed; wherefore it is likened unto their being nourished by the Gentiles, and being carried in their arms and upon their shoulders." (1 Nephi 22:7-8.)

The Lord added this further promise:

"Wherefore my beloved brethren, thus saith our God, I will afflict thy seed by the hand of the Gentiles, nevertheless I will soften the hearts of the Gentiles that they shall be like a father to them; wherefore the Gentiles shall be blessed and numbered among the house of Israel." (2 Nephi 10:18.)

Nothing in history is more fascinating, more emotionally moving, than the life span of the descendants of Laman and Lemuel, extending over a hectic period of some twenty-six centuries.

It portrays every phase of human life, for these peoples went from horizon to horizon in human experience. War, peace, savagery and culture, exploitations on land and sea, love and hate, achievement and degradation, divine worship and sensual idolatry—it is all there, an age-long saga that began with two errant brothers.

However, it will end in the brilliance of millennial glory when Christ comes to fulfill every promise made of old by the prophets of God.

THE LAMANITE
MISSIONS

CHAPTER THREE

Surprising as it may seem, missionary work has been one of the major factors in the long history of the Lamanite people. It was so with the Nephites and the Lamanites anciently. It is equally so today.

The Lord has spared no effort to bring the light of the gospel to the descendants of Laman and Lemuel.

In ancient America the Nephites made frequent and extensive efforts to convert "the seed of my brethren," and at times the reverse was true. There were periods when the Lamanites were more righteous than the Nephites, and they set an example of obedience to their white brethren.

We read with great admiration the story of Helaman and his two thousand young men, and we remember that these stripling warriors reached great heights of valor because of the teachings of their mothers who were converts from among the Lamanites.

The labors of the sons of King Mosiah were exceptional, filled with miracles, bringing in large congregations of believing Lamanites.

Nephite efforts to convert their brethren continued over the centuries except for periods when the Nephites became more evil than the Lamanites.

In those instances, the believing Lamanites endeavored to bring the Nephites back to the fold. Some were successful. Others were not.

One of the notable cases of this kind was the ministration of Samuel the Lamanite. Little is known of him except for his dramatic appearance on the walls of Zarahemla. It was five years before the birth of the Savior when Samuel made his appearance.

"The Nephites did remain in wickedness, yea in great wickedness while the Lamanites did observe strictly to keep the commandments of God according to the law of Moses."

Samuel came into the land and began to preach to the people, calling on them to repent, but in anger they cast him out of the city. He was about to return to his own country when the voice of the Lord commanded him to return and give the people further warning.

The Nephites would not allow him to enter the gates so he climbed on the city wall, and declared, "I, Samuel the Lamanite, do speak the words of the Lord which he doth put into my heart."

And then he predicted:

1. "Four hundred years pass not away save the sword of justice falleth upon this people." It was a clear prediction of the final battles at the Hill Cumorah and the annihilation of the Nephite race.

2. "Five more years cometh and behold then cometh the Son of God to redeem all those who shall believe on his name." This directly foretold the birth of the Savior in Bethlehem.

But a sign would be given the Nephites of that day: "Therefore there shall be one day and a night and a day and this shall be unto you for a sign. . . . And it shall be the night before he is born."

3. "Behold as I said unto you concerning another sign of his death," he foretold the stupendous cataclysm to fall upon the land during a period of three days and nights of darkness and three hours of fire, earthquake and tempest, all of this to come at the time of the Lord's crucifixion in Palestine.

4. "And now behold, saith the Lord concerning the people of the Nephites, if they will not repent and observe to do my will, I will utterly destroy them saith the Lord because of their unbelief." (Helaman, chapters 14 and 15.) This looked toward the annihilation at Cumorah.

The majority of the Nephites who heard Samuel's message completely rejected him, and many tried to shoot him with arrows as he stood on the wall. But the Lord protected him, and when he had finished his message he escaped and disappeared.

Another major mission of the Nephites to the Lamanites before the coming of Christ was undertaken by two sons of Helaman named Nephi and Lehi.

They went among the Lamanites who lived in the vicinity of the great city Zarahemla.

As Nephi and Lehi moved into the land of Nephi they were seized by the Lamanites who controlled that area and cast into prison, where they remained for "many days" without food. They were condemned to death, and when the guards came to slay them "it came to pass that Nephi and Lehi were encircled about as if by fire, even insomuch that they durst not lay their hands upon them for fear lest they should be burned. Nevertheless, Nephi and Lehi were not burned; and they were as standing in the midst of fire and were not burned." (Helaman 5:23.)

When Nephi and Lehi realized that they were surrounded by fire, and that it did not burn them, they knew the Lord was with them and they no longer feared.

A soft but piercing voice was heard, saying: "Repent ye, repent ye, and seek no more to destroy my servants whom I have sent unto you to declare good tidings." (Helaman 5:29.)

A former Nephite who once had been a believer but had dissented to the Lamanites was there. Through the darkness he saw the faces of Nephi and Lehi in the bright light, shining "even as the faces of angels."

This man cried out to the multitude and told them to look toward Nephi and Lehi.

"And they said unto the man: Behold, what do all these things mean, and who is it with whom these men do converse?" (Verse 38.)

The Spirit of God entered the hearts of the Lamanites and they were converted. There were three hundred of them in this place, "and it came to pass that they did go forth, and did minister unto the people, declaring throughout all the regions round about all the things which they had heard and seen, insomuch that the more part of the Lamanites were convinced of them, because of the greatness of the evidences which they had received.

"And as many as were convinced did lay down their weapons of war, and also their hatred and the tradition of their fathers.

"And it came to pass that they did yield up unto the Nephites the lands of their possession." (Helaman 5:50-52.)

13

THEIR
GREATEST MISSION

The most extensive mission to the Lamanites, and the most successful, began with the appearance of the Savior in ancient America.

It will be remembered that wide destruction came to the western hemisphere at the time of the crucifixion of the Lord. For about three hours indescribable tempests, fires, and earthquakes swept over the whole land.

Cities burned, some were buried by mountains falling upon them, others were submerged in the sea. Deep darkness descended and remained for three days. It was so heavy with vapor that no light could be struck nor fires kindled, and the people who survived the cataclysms of nature were left in dire distress for the entire period.

In the thirty-fourth year after the birth of Christ and on the fourth day of the first month of the year there "arose a great storm, such an one as never had been known in all the land." (3 Nephi 8:5.)

When the tempests stopped and there was quiet, but while the darkness yet remained, a voice from heaven was heard. It was the beginning of this greatest of all missionary efforts. God himself spoke, making a mighty appeal to the people who had survived, urging them to repent and believe in the Lord. The voice told them that they had been spared because they were not as wicked as those who had been slain but that, even so, they needed great repentance.

"Wo, wo, wo unto this people; wo unto the inhabitants of the whole earth except they repent," said the voice.

And then came this startling declaration:

"Behold, I am Jesus Christ, the Son of God. I created the heavens and the earth, and all things that in them are. I was with the Father from the beginning. I am in the Father, and the Father in me; and in me hath the Father glorified his name.

"I came unto my own, and my own received me not. And the scriptures concerning my coming are fulfilled.

"And as many as have received me, to them have I given to become the sons of God; and even so will I to as many as shall believe on my name, for behold by me redemption cometh, and in me is the law of Moses fulfilled.

"I am the light and the life of the world. I am Alpha and Omega, the beginning and the end." (3 Nephi 9:15-18.)

The people who heard were struck with astonishment, and they ceased weeping for the loss of their relatives. Silence reigned both on earth and in heaven. Then came the voice once more:

"O ye house of Israel whom I have spared, how oft will I gather you as a hen gathereth her chickens under her wings, if ye will repent and return unto me with full purpose of heart." (3 Nephi 10:6.)

At the end of the three days of darkness, light returned. The people left their shelters and looked about, surveying the change that had come to the landscape.

Then came another voice from heaven. They could not understand the tongue in which it spoke. A second time it came; again they could not understand. A third time, and it was in their own language. The voice said:

"Behold, My Beloved Son, in whom I am well pleased, in whom I have glorified my name—hear ye him." (3 Nephi 11:7.)

The people looked toward heaven and saw a figure in white descending. At first they thought it was an angel. Then as He reached the earth and stood before them, this glorious figure said:

"Behold, I am Jesus Christ whom the prophets testified shall come into the world."

The people remembered that their prophets had foretold the coming of Jesus to their continent. They fell to the earth in fear and astonishment. Then the Lord said:

"Arise and come forth unto me, that ye may thrust your hands into my side, and also that ye may feel the prints of the nails in my hands and in my feet, that ye may know that I am the God of Israel, and the God of the whole earth, and have been slain for the sins of the world.

"And it came to pass that the multitude went forth, and thrust their hands into his side, and did feel the prints of the nails in his hands and in his feet; and this they did do,

15

going forth one by one until they had all gone forth, and did see with their eyes and did feel with their hands, and did know of a surety and did bear record, that it was he, of whom it was written by the prophets, that should come.

"And when they had all gone forth and had witnessed for themselves, they did cry out with one accord, saying:

"Hosanna! Blessed be the name of the Most High God! And they did fall down at the feet of Jesus, and did worship him." (3 Nephi 11:14-17.)

The Savior began immediately to teach His gospel. He called twelve disciples and gave them power to baptize. He taught that all believers must be baptized, and He explained by what mode it should be done.

The ministry of the Savior converted all who came to see Him. After His ascension into heaven, the disciples whom He had appointed continued their labors.

Within about a year—in the thirty-fifth year after the birth of Jesus—His disciples had organized the Church in "all the lands round about."

There was no contention. Peace reigned everywhere.

Thus was accomplished the greatest missionary effort on record, when, through the personal ministry of the resurrected Savior, the entire population of the land became converts, Nephites and Lamanites alike. Their peace lasted for two hundred years.

THE APPEAL
AT CUMORAH

CHAPTER FIVE

Following two hundred years of peace, wickedness again raised its head. Men and women alike began to stray from the Church. Selfishness reappeared. People withheld their properties and broke up the common order. Rich and poor again appeared among the people.

Grievous sin grew worse year by year. The wicked took upon themselves the name of Lamanites. The more righteous resumed the name of Nephites.

But it was not long until the Nephites were more wicked than the Lamanites. Both factions organized armies and severe wars were fought, with heavy losses on both sides.

Among the Nephites a great young warrior arose. His name was Mormon. He led the Nephites to victory repeatedly, but when wickedness continued to spread among them, in disgust he refused to lead them any more.

Mormon made great appeals to the Nephites to repent and seek the protection of God. They would not. As a result battles were lost and hosts of people died.

There is no record that during this time any missionary work was done among the Lamanites. Enmity was universal, leaving no room for such a labor.

Mormon knew that the end was near for his nation. The people had been told repeatedly that destruction would come if they failed to live the gospel. Yet they denounced their prophets and went on in their iniquity.

The Lamanites were more numerous than the Nephites and continued to drive them back.

Heeding the command of the Lord, Mormon began to make a history of his people. Over the centuries prophets and other good men chosen of the Lord had kept careful records engraved on many metal plates.

Mormon, now custodian of all those records, began to abridge them, taking the sacred history of his people from the time of Lehi and making one volume of the work.

Losing battle after battle, and having no adequate leadership, the Nephites again pleaded with Mormon to command their armies. He responded, and he continued to lead them until the nation was destroyed, himself included.

The Lamanites steadily drove the Nephites northward, finally reaching the area of what is now western New York state. Around a hill called Cumorah the last pitched battles were fought.

Combat was hand to hand, one man against one man, with sword or ax or spear. Defense was with shields as well as their fighting weapons. Loss of life was enormous.

Mormon had a faithful son whose name was Moroni. He helped his father with the sacred records which had been engraved on gold plates. Moroni also was one of the generals of the army, under the direction of his father.

In a matter of days a quarter of a million fighting men were slain among the Nephites at the Hill Cumorah.

Knowing that his own death was imminent, Mormon delivered the sacred records to Moroni, his son, for final safe-keeping.

Moroni alone of all the Nephites survived the battles and hid himself for safety. In hiding he continued to write the record begun by his father. He wrote directly to the Lamanites and appealed to them to repent and accept Christ as their Savior, expecting that at some future time the record would be given to them.

His plan was to bury the record in the ground, whence it would come forth in the latter days by the command of God. But before placing it in its hiding place, he wrote one final appeal, to both the Gentiles and the Lamanites, and said:

"Behold, I would exhort you that when ye shall read these things, if it be wisdom in God that ye should read them, that ye would remember how merciful the Lord hath been unto the children of men, from the creation of Adam even down unto the time that ye shall receive these things, and ponder it in your hearts.

"And when ye shall receive these things, I would exhort you that ye would ask God, the Eternal Father, in the name of Christ if these things are not true; and if ye shall ask with a sincere heart, with real intent, having faith in Christ, he will manifest the truth of it unto you, by the power of the Holy Ghost.

"And by the power of the Holy Ghost ye may know the truth of all things. . . .

"And again, if ye by the grace of God are perfect in Christ, and deny not his power, then are ye sanctified in Christ by the grace of God, through the shedding of the blood of Christ, which is in the convenant of the Father unto the remission of your sins, that ye become holy, without spot.

"And now I bid unto all, farewell. I soon go to rest in the paradise of God, until my spirit and body shall again reunite and I am brought forth triumphant through the air, to meet you before the pleasing bar of the great Jehovah, the Eternal Judge of both quick and dead. Amen." (Moroni 10:1-5, 33-34.)

Thus ended the efforts of the true servants of God to carry on a missionary effort in ancient times in America. Now these endeavors must rest with the record which they had written, buried in the ground, and left to the mercies of God.

As Isaiah said, this ancient people, now through this record, could only speak out of the ground, "low out of the dust." But even so their testimonies are strong, filled with the Holy Spirit, and bold in their affirmations of the divine Sonship of Christ. (Isaiah 29.)

PART II

THE
GREAT
DISPERSION

THE LAMANITE'S PRAYER
Charles W. Penrose

Great Spirit, Listen to the Red
    Man's wail!
Thou hast the power to help him
    in his woe.
Thy mighty arm was never
    known to fail,
Great Chieftain, save him from
    the paleface foe.

O, shall our nation, once so great,
    decay?
Our children perish, and our
    chieftains die?
Great Spirit, help! Thy glorious
    power display.
Destroy our foes! O! Hear the
    Indian's cry.

THE TRAIL
OF TEARS

What do we say about a man who fights a marauder to the death to save the lives of his wife and little children?

If he is a white man, he is called a hero, a courageous husband and father.

And if he did this in the cause of liberty and justice, he would be called a patriot, a lover of home and country. Such men are honored with monuments, posthumous decorations for bravery, and a place in history with other benefactors of the nation.

But if the man is an Indian, what do we say?

In American history he has been called a savage, a murderer, a plunderer, a renegade, and an impediment to the westward expansion of the nation.

There is nothing in the history of the United States quite as heartbreaking and tragic as the treatment the white man accorded the red man as our borders were moved toward the setting sun.

It was a detailed fulfillment of Nephi's vision in which "I beheld the wrath of God that it was upon the seed of my brethren, and they were scattered before the Gentiles and were smitten." (1 Nephi 13:14.)

To the invasion of the lands they had held for many generations they reacted in a perfectly normal way, even as the white man has done in other circumstances.

They fought for their homes and hunting grounds, their farms, their all, as adventurers and land-hungry settlers routed them from their possessions.

Where was mercy? Where was justice? Where was any trace of Christian consideration of one human being for another?

25

But are Indians really human in the sense that white men are? Were they in truth savages, ruthless and murderous down through the years?

White men robbed the Indians of their rights. They were in the way of the westward expansion of the new nation, it is true. But must there have been an extermination order? "They must move or be destroyed!"

In their eagerness to expand westward, the Americans of the early nineteenth century violated every principle set forth by their own leaders in their own Declaration of Independence.

Had they not written in all earnestness the principles for which their own compatriots had fought and died?

> We hold these truths to be self-evident:
> That all men are created equal,
> That they are endowed by their Creator
> With certain unalienable rights,
> That among these are Life, Liberty
> And the pursuit of Happiness.
> (From the Declaration of Independence.)

But after writing that, and fighting a war to defend it, they overran and in many cases massacred their Indian neighbors to seize their lands, to plant more plantations, to grow more cotton and make more money.

Who were these Indians, foreigners with no just claim to their lands? They had occupied them for generations! They were not inhuman creatures who delighted in scalping helpless settlers. Frequently they showed a depth of human kindness to these white settlers who fell into difficulty.

Were they not the original owners of the lands on which they now lived and where they had been since before there were any American colonies, even before Columbus saw these shores?

This was where the red men made their homes, raised their families, and taught their little ones to survive in the wilderness. Here they hunted their game and raised their maize. Were their rights not as unalienable as those of their white brothers?

Where was life, liberty, and the pursuit of happiness for them? Were these precious gifts of good government only for white people? Were not the Indians created equal with others?

Did anyone consider that these dwellers in the wilderness were in fact "brothers under the skin," a people made

up of families who loved their homes as other people did, a people who enjoyed these lands before the white men ever saw them? Who could blame them for fighting for their possessions?

And who were these white settlers? The Indians knew them only as interlopers, land grabbers, robbing the red men of all they possessed.

The tragedy was repeated from New England to Florida. Not even the Allegheny mountains could keep these Americans along the seaboard.

In the Southeast one of the most regrettable tragedies took place. It began on a small scale but grew rapidly into a national movement, first centering chiefly in Florida, Georgia, Alabama and Mississippi.

Plantation owners there were hungry for more room to grow cotton. The market was good. Slave labor was cheap. There seemed to be every reason to expand.

But to acquire more land meant to take it from the Indians, because they occupied the very regions the white men wanted. The plantation owners demanded that the Indians move out. They recognized no claim to Indian ownership. To them the area was all virgin territory available and free — that is, free for the white man but not the red.

The matter came to a head with the completion of the Louisiana Purchase, when the vast region west of the Mississippi River, from Mexico to Canada, was acquired from France in 1803.

Then the expansion movement exploded. Plantation owners tried to compel the United States government to solve the "Indian problem." The farmers of Georgia threatened to secede from the Union if they could not have their way.

When Andrew Jackson was elected president of the United States, he pushed through Congress an Indian Removal Bill on May 28, 1830. It empowered the president to exchange with the Indians lands west of the river for what they occupied east of the river. When the Indians resisted, the haughty Jackson ordered the army to "get them out."

The Choctaws, the Creeks, and the Chicasaws began to move. The Cherokees appealed to the United States Supreme Court for a decision, and Justice John Marshall ruled that there was no constitutional basis for driving the Indians from their lands.

This angered Jackson, who refused to accept the decision. He sent the army against the unfortunate red men with extermination orders.

"This imperious ruling came to apply wherever the white men cared to explore," says Alistair Cooke in his *America.* (Knopf, c. 1973, p. 170.)

"In the end, the major part of all of the tribes were removed to new homes in the present state of Oklahoma, some of the bands going peaceably, some in chains, and most of them under the watchful eyes of troops who prodded them on. . . .

"The march west in 1838 and 1839—known as the 'Trail of Tears'—was bitter. Nearly one quarter of the Cherokees died of starvation, disease, and hardship, as troops pushed the Indians across the South to Oklahoma. A band of several hundred Cherokees evaded detection in the North Carolina mountains; their descendants still live there." (*Collier's Encyclopedia,* Vol. 12, p. 685.)

One hundred thousand Indians fell victims to this outrage.

The National Geographic Society quotes the French traveler Count Alexis de Tocqueville, who stood on the banks of the Mississippi as a band of Choctaws crossed over:

"The Indians had their families with them, and they brought in their train the wounded and the sick, with children newly born, and old men on the verge of death. They possessed neither tents nor wagons, but only their arms and some provisions." (D'Arcy McNickle in *The World of the American Indian,* p. 311; c. 1974, National Geographic Society.)

It was a sad day indeed, for both the whites and the Indians.

This was typical of Indian wars from Mexico to Canada and from Florida to California.

The Indian affairs of the United States government were placed in the hands of the army, with orders to fight, to drive, and to confine these now hated and feared aborigines to reservations.

In the Southwest, Mexicans who were but recently defeated in their war with the United States stirred up the Indians at Taos, New Mexico, as revenge for their loss in the war, inciting another massacre.

In the Great Basin impoverished Gosiutes and Paiutes annoyed the trappers, "and the impatient Americans retaliated by shooting the defenseless Indians almost as sport." (*Colliers Encyclopedia,* Vol. 12, p. 687.)

There was Custer's Last Stand in June of 1876. Two hundred and twenty-five men, including Custer himself,

were wiped out by enraged Indians led by Crazy Horse. The massacre stunned the nation.

And then there was Wounded Knee, in South Dakota, where U.S. troops killed three hundred men, women and children of the Sioux tribe in 1890.

This was one of the blackest tragedies of all the Indian wars. The vicious attack, even upon helpless women and little children, equaled the worst the Indians had ever attempted. It was plain, ugly massacre. The frozen bodies of the victims were subsequently stacked like cordwood and buried in a common grave.

Great leaders arose among the Indians. White men regarded them as outlaws and enemies, but these chieftains merely defended themselves and their families.

Sitting Bull of the Little Big Horn expressed the Indian feelings when he said:

"You have taken our lands and made us outcasts."

Red Cloud of the Oglala Sioux expressed it, too, when he complained: "Are sacred graves to be plowed for corn? Dakotas, I am for war."

Geronimo of the Apaches said, "I think I am a good man, but all over the world they say I am a bad man." He merely fought for his rights and his people.

Chief Joseph of the Nez Perce grieved deeply when the whites broke their treaties and crowded into Indian lands. He said, "My heart is sick and sad. From where the sun now stands I will fight no more."

The *National Geographic* writers expressed it like this:

"The Indian wars make for sensational reading, but more important is the story of the Indian will to survive and to preserve his own sense of moral order.

"The Indian fought when he had to, and fought well, even when outgunned. But the harmony he prized as the proper relationship between men and the universe was not achieved in battle. . . .

"The thread of continuity which bound the Indian experience together through time and across geographical space, was the vision of a native America free of domination by the outsider — the white man." (*The World of the American Indian*, National Geographic Society, c. 1974, p. 352.)

One horrible example of the duplicity of the U.S. officials in dealing with the Indians came in 1851.

Thirty-six miles from Fort Laramie, near what the Indians called Horse Creek, a gathering of Indian tribes was held under the direction of Thomas Fitzpatrick, Indian agent for that area.

"By the waters of the swift-flowing stream the Sioux were meeting in peace with their ancient enemies, the Crows, while the Arikara, Cheyenne, Assinboine, Arapaho and Gros Ventre tribes, as well as delegates from several others, were engaged in days of council, ceremony and feasting.

"In all some 10,000 red men were gathered at the call of the Great Father and his representatives, Thomas Fitzpatrick and Colonel David D. Mitchell, to make permanent peace among the tribes and agree formally to the free passage of the white man's wagon trains across their hunting grounds." (*Story of the Great American West*, Reader's Digest, c. 1977, p. 210.)

The government offered to pay fifty thousand dollars a year in supplies to the tribes if they would agree to divide among themselves designated sections of the Great Plains and be willing to restrict all their activities to these areas, including hunting, fishing, and camping.

It was not believed that the Indians, who knew very little English, understood these conditions. After days of discussion among themselves, and not knowing fully what they were doing, the Indians agreed to the terms.

Hardly had the treaties been made than Congress reneged and failed to provide the promised compensation as set forth in the treaties.

"The tribes were forced to continue far-ranging hunting expeditions that put them in sharp contention with one another for the dwindling supply of game. By 1853 Tom Fitzpatrick was deploring the Indians' plight.

"They were, he wrote, 'in abject want of food half the year. . . . The travel upon the road drives the buffalo off or else confines them to a narrow path during the period of emigration and the different tribes are forced to contend with hostile nations. . . . Their women are pinched with want and their children constantly cry with hunger." (Ibid. p. 211.)

THEY GO
THEIR WAYS

As the ancient Israelites suffered a dispersion which sprinkled them among all the nations, so the descendants of Laman and Lemuel were sifted over the vast areas of the western hemisphere. They are found from pole to pole.

Millions developed nations in South America. It is estimated that today there are still 36 million pure-blooded Indians on that continent, primarily in the west, central, and northern parts. Other millions in Mexico and Central America developed high degrees of civilization long before the coming of the Spanish conquerors.

Some sailed into the broad Pacific and became the Polynesians. Those who went to the far north intermarried with Asiatics who apparently crossed the Bering Sea on the Aleutian chain and became Eskimos. Others are found in the Antarctic.

Many populated the various parts of what is now the United States and Canada and formed numerous tribes with contrasting habits of life.

It is not supposed that all the Lamanites in America were involved in the battles at the Hill Cumorah. Many never went there. They were separated by formidable distances, living as they did in what is now Peru and Bolivia, Mexico and Central America, Arizona, Alaska, and British Columbia, not to mention those who went to Hawaii, Samoa, Easter Island, Tonga, Tahiti, and New Zealand.

Varied patterns of tribal cultures developed as the Lamanites occupied the western hemisphere. Geography had much to do with their mode of life. Some tilled the soil and grew crops, even with irrigation. and domesticated animals.

Others were hunters who roamed the forests and the plains in search of game. Some became farmers and basket makers, skilled craftsmen in the use of metal, makers of fine textiles, jewelry, and pottery. They built pyramids, astronomical observatories, temples, and one city nearly three miles above sea level in Peru.

Scholars designate the Indians' North American basic cultural areas as follows:

Meso-America, in Mexico and Central America.

The Great Southwest, chiefly in Arizona and New Mexico.

The Intermediate group, referring mainly to California and the Intermountain region.

The Northeast, occupied by tribes which included the great Iroquois League, extending through New York, the Great Lakes area, and New England.

The Pacific Northwest, including Washington, Oregon, and the Vancouver area.

The Arctic, taking in the Yukon, Alaska, and the Aleutian chain.

In South America they were placed in four categories: the Andean, the Circum-Caribbean, the Tropical Forest, and Marginal tribes.

Actually there was a close relationship between Meso-America and the Andean region. It is known as the "bi-continental core of development." This combined region was far ahead of any other part of the hemisphere in both density of population and advancement in the arts, in political processes and mineral wealth. Archaeologists believe that their advanced mode of living may be traced back as far as 500 B.C., equalling anything Europe had to offer at the time of the Spanish conquest.

It is interesting that in this same area native American cultivated plants first appeared, the most important being beans and maize.

"Domestication of plants and wild animals was of great importance in the development of New World cultures. With the possible exception of the gourd and cotton, the domesticated plants of the New World are indigenous species unrelated to plants of the Old World.

"Recent botanical investigations point to the conclusion that plants such as maize, sweet potatoes, peppers, peanuts, manioc, and tobacco, which are each represented by a single species, are of South American origin. . . .

"Other plants such as squash, beans, tomatoes, and cotton, which are represented by two or more species, may have been domesticated independently in South America and Central America. Still other plants such as coca, the white potato, quinoa, and oca seem to be Andean in origin." (*Encyclopedia Americana*, 1958, Vol. 15, p. 48.)

The sweet potato was unknown to Europeans until the discovery of America, but before that time it was widely distributed among the Polynesian Islands. (R. B. Dixon, *The Problem of the Sweet Potato in Polynesia*, quoted by Hyerdahl.)

Peruvian cotton species and gourds were transported to the Polynesian Islands by pre-Columbian voyagers. (Hyerdahl, *The Secret of Easter Island*, McNally, p. 375-6.)

The coconut palm had its origin in America and was introduced into Polynesia "long ago." (Copeland, *The Coconut*, London.) The pineapple is native to Peru, Mexico, and Brazil. (Hyerdahl, *American Indians in the Pacific*, Ruskin House, London, p. 466-467.) The papaya was native to tropical America and was taken to Polynesia, as were the "hust tomato" and other foods mentioned by Hyerdahl, in which he quotes various authorities.

The marginal tribes extended from the eastern highlands of Brazil across the Chaco and on down into the tip of South America. They were nomadic hunters.

The Alacauf and Yahgam of the Chilean archipelago and the Ona and Teheulche of Patagonia (Argentina) are considered the most primitive Indians in all of South America.

In the area of the United States the main prehistoric cultures were the Anasazi, the Hohokam and Mogollon.

The Anasazi people were the basket makers and the builders of peublos. They lived mostly in the plateau areas of Arizona and New Mexico and were farmers.

The Hohokams centered in the southern Arizona deserts and were later known as the Pima and Papago. They also farmed.

The Mogollons lived in east central Arizona and west central New Mexico, mostly in the mountains.

The basket-maker period extended from A.D. 100 to A.D. 700. These people domesticated turkeys and maize and were makers of fine pottery. They were primarily farmers.

The Pueblos (A.D. 700 to A.D. 1050) created pueblo towns such as those at Mesa Verde and Chaco Canyon.

Villages of historic pueblo people included the Zunis,

the Hopis, and the Rio Grande, as well as the Taos, San Juan and Santa Clara Indians.

The Hopi Indians were among the advanced tribes of the Southwest. They occupied mesas northwest of Flagstaff, Arizona. Known historically as Moqui or Moki, they lived in multi-storied homes made of native stone and adobe.

These people had a matriarchal system of government. However, the men controlled the ceremonial activities. The tribes were autonomous, with no central chief, each tribe having its own leadership.

The hogan-dwelling Navajos are often seen in the Arizona and Southern Utah deserts herding their few sheep or trying to encourage corn to grow on the arid and almost sterile soil of that region.

Closely related to the Apache, they intermarried with Pueblos, Shoshones, and the Yumans.

This tribe also is strongly matriarchal. According to Dr. Washington Matthews, one of the foremost students on the Navajo, a man belongs to the clan of his mother and may not marry a woman of his own clan.

The Navajo are peace-loving and industrious. They make good laborers but are very slowly developing their agricultural pursuits.

The tribes of the Southwest retained their culture longer than other groups. The arriving white explorers and conquerors hardly disturbed the native customs of the Navajo, Pueblo, and Apache.

Indians of the Pacific Northwest are clearly different from most other tribes. They had a distinct development of social and economic life, placing great emphasis upon the gathering of wealth and also on its distribution. Thus they dealt extensively in various foods, shell-currency, slaves, and sheets of native copper.

Due consideration must be given to the possibilities of migration across the Bering Sea along the Aleutian chain of islands. There is every reason to suppose that in the remote past the sea was shallower there than it is now, and that instead of islands there actually was a "land bridge" connecting Siberia and Alaska.

The languages of the Indians in both North and South America developed into a veritable babel of tongues. In South America there were 250 different languages classified into 40 linguistic stocks. Most prominent was Quechua, which was the accepted language of the Incas, who suppressed the local

dialects of peoples whom they conquered, forcing their subjects to learn Quechua.

It is estimated that there were between five hundred
and six hundred different languages spoken among the
various North American tribes. "A reasonable consensus
today distinguishes 18 language families, each containing
from one to more than 20 languages," according to Wallace
L. Chafe, writing in *The World of the American Indian*, for
National Geographic Society (p. 150).

THE MAYA
AND THE INCA

Lamanites deteriorated in many parts of the hemisphere as they lowered their standards of living, but in the Mexico-Peru region it was quite the opposite.

There they developed one of the greatest civilizations of their time, anywhere. They were skilled at writing, they knew astronomy, they made accurate calendars, they were adept at beautiful textiles, and they knew how to make permanent colors, some of which are still bright.

They built good highways, erected temples, and worked in metals, particularly gold.

The Mayans in Central America and Yucatan reached the greatest heights of civilization in the west. They built beautiful cities and large pyramids and developed an advanced system of agriculture.

They produced new strains of various plants and terraced the hillsides to save both soil and water.

The National Geographic publication known as *The Mysterious Maya*, by George E. and Gene S. Stuart (c. 1977) indicates that although the Mayan civilization goes back many centuries, it reached its height between A.D. 250 and A.D. 900.

"During those six and a half centuries the Maya created one of the most distinguished civilizations of all antiquity. . . ." (p. 38-39.)

The accuracy of their calendar and the evidence of careful astronomical observation has been an amazement even to the greatest modern scholars.

Evidence that man in the Mayan culture went far back into the ages is expressed in this valuable book.

"Evidence of another house virtually identical to ours at Coba is among the earliest traces of man in the Mayan area. That house stood almost 4,500 years ago in what is now northern Belize." (Ibid. p. 22.)

Norman Hammond of Rutgers University, associated with the team from National Geographic, "found something more at the bottom of his pit. The earliest pottery of Cuello lies there on bedrock, and radio carbon readings from charred wood insist persuasively that it dates from about 2600 B.C., earlier than any other sherds yet excavated in Mesoamerica." (Ibid.)

This publication says that the Maya today number about two million and that they speak some twenty-four highland and lowland languages related about as closely as are the various Romance languages. (Ibid.)

The greatest centers of their civilization were in the lowlands, where they built cities like Tikal, covering an area of fifty square miles with a population of fifty thousand. This city was at its height at A.D. 800.

At Vera Cruz archaeological findings indicate a presence of well-developed man as long ago as six thousand years.

Diggings there have produced remains of the giant sloth, the horse, and the mastodon dating back, the scientists estimate, fourteen thousand years.

The Aztecs, the Olmecs, and the Zapotecs all contributed to the advance in ancient living.

These people generally were religious. They believed in the Creator, they had faith in the life hereafter, and some of them taught that death was simply a birth to a new life.

However, human sacrifice was common among them, as of course it was in other parts of the world, even going back to the time of Abraham in the Old World.

It is recalled that in Book of Mormon times the Lamanites resorted to human sacrifice, a custom obviously handed down to the Meso-Americans.

The Inca empire was one of the greatest known in ancient America. It is believed that there were as many as six million people under its rule.

The Incas reached the height of their civilization about A.D. 1500. Their leaders were believed to have been white men, survivors of a royal line from earlier times. They thought they were related to the sun, and they claimed the throne by divine right.

The empire was three thousand miles long, from Colombia to Chile. A direct administrative line of government extended from the throne to the smallest village. All important military and governmental officials were chosen from among the descendants of former emperors, power thus being concentrated within a small group.

The farm land was divided into three parts, for the support respectively of the state, the priesthood, and the people at large. Everyone was required to work on farms, roads, or other public works. Taxes were paid in labor.

Like the ancient Greeks, the Incas transplanted thousands of people from one area to another, especially after a new conquest, to protect their government and insure loyalty among their new subjects.

All aspects of the subjects' lives were rigidly controlled. The Incas had elaborate highway systems, two main roads stretching the length of their empire, one on the coast and the other in the highlands. Along these highways post houses and inns were built for the convenience of the travelers. Post houses were only three miles apart, the inns fifteen.

The Incas built elaborate irrigation systems. Sometimes their ditches were cut through solid rock or carried along sheer cliffs on stone aqueducts. They excelled in engineering and agriculture. Stone-faced agricultural terraces were built over many of the sloping areas, descending to the valley floor.

They constructed palaces, temples, and fortresses. One of their chief cities was Machu Pichu, fifteen thousand feet high in the Andes. They were competent weavers and skilled workers in metals and pottery.

These chapters are not intended to go into great detail regarding ancient peoples but seek merely to give a glimpse of the varied tribes and modes of life of the Lamanites during the period when the gospel was not on the earth.

THE OLMECS
AND THE AZTECS

CHAPTER NINE

Meso-American civilization reached its zenith with the Maya, but the Aztec holds a prominent place in early Mexican history because it was under Aztec rule that the Spanish conquest came.

But earlier civilizations preceded both. The Olmecs are believed to have risen about 1200 B.C. The earliest-known farming villages were probably created by them in the valley of Oaxaca about that time.

The Olmecs settled San Lorenzo, Vera Cruz, between 1200 and 900 B.C. Archaeologists believe that they appeared suddenly. Their origin is not known. They began establishing religious centers, the main one being at San Lorenzo dated about 1150 B.C.

They built mounds, plazas, and reservoirs. They created great sculptured pieces of art, some classed as colossal in size. Religion seemed to be a center theme in the lives of the Olmecs. They believed in the "were-jaguar," a combination of man and jaguar.

The Aztecs were a very advanced people. They too were great builders, and they erected beautiful palaces, strong arsenals, and religious centers. Their religion was polytheistic and permitted the worship of the local deities known to the people whom they conquered. To this extent there was freedom of religion; human sacrifice was included in their rituals.

They were students of astronomy and made a calendar which is highly regarded by scientists. The Sun Stone, or calendar of the Aztecs, is twelve feet across and weighs twenty tons.

A complex but accurate calendar was kept by the Zapotecs also.

"The Zapotecs of the 16th century kept two calendars, one secular and the other ritual. The secular calendar of 365 days (yza) was divided into 18 'moons' of 20 days and one period of five days." (Joyce Marcus in "Zapotec Writing," *Scientific Monthly*, Feb. 1980.)

The great pyramids of the sun and the moon near Mexico City are among the nation's chief tourist attractions.

POLYNESIANS AND
MOUND BUILDERS

CHAPTER TEN

For nearly a century anthropologists and historians have conjectured over the origin of the Polynesian peoples. Some suggest that the Maoris especially are a combination of ancestors who came from both east and west, and particularly from the Melanesian Islands. But both tradition and blood tie them to a Lamanitish origin. As elsewhere, there may be some mixture with other races, but Laman and Lemuel seem to dominate.

Some suggest the settlers of those warm islands of the Pacific came from the Far East. Others believe they came from the area of Peru or from the Vancouver region. There is no agreement among the scholars.

One thing many do unite on is that both white and dark peoples lived at the same time on nearly all of the islands of the Polynesian chain, from Easter Island and Hawaii down to the tip of New Zealand. There is evidence that in the distant past white and dark people lived in America also, as for instance among the Incas.

Some say that the islands probably were not discovered until about A.D. 500 and that the first major settlements came in about A.D. 800 and most likely from American shores.

Most myths of the natives trace their origin to the east, a place of high mountains. Some of them tell of trees that lose their leaves for half of each year, and of ice on the waters making it possible for men to "walk on the water."

41

Genealogies are traced back to the land of high mountains, and to a large degree they harmonize with the mythology of the natives.

The migrants who came from the "high mountains" to the east (America), seem to have landed first on either Easter Island, Hawaii, or both at about the same time.

An interesting legend indicates that those who came to Easter Island arrived not in canoes adrift in a storm but in big ships. This is borne out by evidences found on Easter Island, including heavy materials which were hauled in long ago, not being native to the island, and which were far too big and heavy for any canoe.

The Book of Mormon speaks of Hagoth and his big ships, in which he carried on a commercial enterprise with "the land northward." (Alma 63.)

Part of his business was in lumber taken north from the southland, because the land northward had been denuded of its trees. The traffic also seems to have included cement and other enduring building materials, for such were largely used there.

President Joseph F. Smith announced his belief that the New Zealanders "are some of Hagoth's people and there is no perhaps about it."

When President David O. McKay dedicated the New Zealand temple, he spoke of the Polynesians as descendants of Father Lehi. (*Early America and the Polynesians*, Paul R. Cheesman, p. 14.)

Construction of great pyramids characterized the early peoples of Mexico, Central America, and South America. Pyramids of almost identical structure both in plan and material, if not in size, are found in Polynesia.

Stone highways of the pre-Inca period are found to be duplicated in some of the Pacific Islands. Giant statues like those found particularly in the land of the Incas are discovered in the Polynesian Islands.

Fortifications built on the islands remind us of those described in the Book of Mormon.

It is well established that on mainland America in early times there were both white- and dark-skinned peoples. That some of them came to Polynesia is well attested.

Mummies of white people with blond or red hair have been found and photographed, as seen in Thor Hyerdahl's remarkable book *American Indians in the Pacific*.

As relics of an unknown nation of Lamanites, there are thousands of mysterious mounds in a wide area of eastern and southern United States. They are the work of "the mound builders," so identified for want of a better name.

Some formed a base for temples, others are burial mounds, and some apparently were part of a defense system. Present-day Indian peoples are not believed to have been associated with these vast structures, which were built most likely by an earlier tribe not known now to the scholars. Some theories credit the Toltecs of Mexico with the construction; some others believe the mounds were built by straying Israelites. But this is mere conjecture.

The first extensive studies of the area were made by the Smithsonian Institution of Washington, D.C. Diggings were made originally in 1882; then they were abandoned for a time, being resumed in 1891.

The earthworks in southern Ohio are credited to the Hopewell group, and by the use of carbon 14 methods these structures have been dated at about the time of Christ.

Mounds at the Hopewell site are in geometric figures such as squares, circles, and octagons, each one covering anywhere from twenty to fifty acres.

In the deposits in Mississippi as many as 1,100 skeletons have been taken from a single mound. Scholars believe the Mississippi group dates to between A.D. 900 and 1100. Artifacts with curious decorations such as crosses, spiders, snakes, weeping eyes, and other symbols have been found there.

Because the figure of the serpent is so prominent in the shape of some mounds as well as in the artifacts, scholars believe the builders worshipped the serpent, and some associate them with the Mexican carvings which exhibit the serpent so prominently.

When Stephen D. Peet wrote his discussion on emblematic mounds for *Prehistoric America* (p. 332), he spoke of the serpent as a symbol among the Chinese, the Persians, the Egyptians, and the Chaldeans. He then said:

"The serpent, twisted in the form of a circle, was a familiar symbol among the Hindoos, Persians, Phoenicians, Egyptians, Britains and the Greeks. The caduceus of Hermes exhibited two serpents wound around a staff, a globe, and wings at the top of the staff."

Mysterious as they are, the mounds at least give evidence of one more level to which the Lamanites drifted as they fell away from the Master's teachings.

ANCIENT
VISITORS

Much is said about the origin of the early inhabitants of the Americas. Many are the theories, but in recent years evidence of unusual visitors from afar has been found.

Men such as Dr. Cyrus H. Gordon, head of the Department of Mediterranean Studies at Brandeis University, an internationally respected scholar, cites instances in his book, *Before Columbus*, of definite links between the Old World and Ancient America.

He speaks of Meso-American ceramic figurines which have been found by the archaeologists showing various types of faces, few if any being American Indian types, such as Aztec or Maya, before A.D. 300.

"Those prior to that date (and many that appear for a thousand years thereafter) belong to other races such as Far Eastern, African Negro, and Caucasian. Among the latter are a number of Mediterranean types, especially Semitic." (*Before Columbus*, p. 22. Crown Publishers, N.Y.)

Alexander Von Wuthenau published a book entitled *Unexpected Faces in Ancient America* in which he reproduces pictures of sculptured faces dated at various periods between 1500 B.C. and A.D. 1500. (Crown Publishers, N.Y.)

Making a strong case for the existence of white men in ancient America, he refers to finds at Copán, Honduras, for example, and produces pictures of monumental stone heads, all with non-Indian features, some with definite Semite features, but others he believes are of Irish or Celtic origin.

He says that some heads have been found with Negroid characteristics. Dr. Gordon says the same.

"The Semitic-looking representations are very numerous in all Mayan regions." Von Wuthenau said, "I do not believe that a better ethnic testimony can be found to prove the presence of Semites in America over a thousand years ago. For me, as an art historian, this one piece [which he illustrates in the book] would be sufficient. Yet I am deliberately presenting an abundance of archaeological evidence in this book so as to satisfy the conscientious investigator as well as any open-minded observer." (*Unexpected Faces*, p. 92.)

And then he proceeds to do as he says. His book is filled with close-up photographs of such faces.

He suggests that some of the Semites could have been Babylonians, since their god, Seth, is mentioned; and he then adds that at least two unmistakable Egyptian hieroglyphs prove conclusively that someone came to these shores who knew the Egyptian language. The glyphs he refers to are in the Museum of Jalapa, Vera Cruz. (Ibid. p. 126.)

Dr. Gordon says that Japanese pottery has been found in Ecuador. There is evidence of migrations from the Mediterranean areas at different times with various lines of Semites, some Phoenicians; also some Carthaginians, as well as Greeks, Etruscans, Romans, and others. (*Before Columbus*, p. 30.)

Gordon speaks of Mayan traditions of white bearded men, including the white Being called Kukulcan, which means the plumed serpent. He says the Incas called him Viracocha.

"These traditions," he continues, "point to white people with beards who crossed the Atlantic and made fundamental contributions to the diffusion of culture from the Mediterranean and Europe to Meso-America and some areas in the northern half of South America as well as parts of the southern half of North America." (Ibid. p. 51.)

He reveals language links between Mesopotamia and Meso-America, as well as many seal cylinders which were common to both areas. He points to the similarity of names in ancient America and Egypt.

There can be little doubt about early migrations to America long before either Columbus or Leif Ericson. It is believed that they came both from across the Atlantic and from over the Pacific.

But none of these visitors remained to become the colonizers of America. The Lord had retained America for His purposes, as shown in the history of both the Jaredite people and the descendants of the prophet Lehi.

The Book of Mormon itself speaks of a mixture of

45

blood, that of Mulek, Lehi, Ishmael, and Zoram, the servant of Laban.

It is possible that there may have been intermarriages with daring seamen who came from over both the Atlantic and the Pacific.

But if there were such marriages, the families were absorbed into the overall Lamanite-Nephite or Jaredite populations.

Facial images of various races as seen in the sculptured pieces certainly indicate a knowledge of foreign peoples. Since it is known that some came, it is altogether likely that some remained and did not attempt a return voyage. If they stayed, in all likelihood they did intermarry with the resident peoples.

If there had been large numbers of other peoples here when the Jaredites came, or when Lehi arrived, certainly the Book of Mormon would have said so.

The land was reserved for the Lord's purposes and for His peoples, and the Book of Mormon provides their histories.

PART III

THE LORD
KEEPS
HIS WORD

THE GLORIOUS DAY
Charles W. Penrose

When the proud Gentile nations
    cease to be,
And earth's redeemed and
    clothed in purity,
When harmless lions with the
    lambkins play,
And man shall cease his fellow
    man to slay,
When noxious weeds and harmful
    plants shall die
And fragrant flowers captivate
    the eye;
When nature's voice in peaceful
    tones shall speak,
Nor earthquakes yawn nor jarring
    thunders break,
When the dead Saints to glorious
    life shall rise,
And loud hosannas charm the
    listening skies:
Then shall the noble Indian race
Dwell with the Savior, face to face,

*With the redeemed shall swell the
grateful song
And ever reign with the immortal
throng.*

THE
"NURSING FATHERS"

CHAPTER TWELVE

Dreadful was the affliction heaped upon the Lamanites by the people of the United States, all of which was predicted. Nevertheless these same "Gentiles" were destined to serve as "nursing fathers and mothers" to the victims of their forced expansion.

This promise is made repeatedly in the Book of Mormon:

"Yea, the kings of the Gentiles shall be nursing fathers unto them, and their queens shall become nursing mothers; wherefore the promises of the Lord are great unto the Gentiles, for he hath spoken it, and who can dispute?" (2 Nephi 10:9.)

"Thus saith the Lord God, Behold I will lift up mine hand to the Gentiles and set up my standard to the people, and they shall bring thy sons in their arms and thy daughters shall be carried upon their shoulders." (2 Nephi 6:6.)

There has been a literal fulfillment of these prophecies, an extensive and generous fulfillment. The much-afflicted red man became a ward of the United States government and later was given his full citizenship as rapidly as he was able to carry such a responsibility. Similar conditions developed in Canada.

In all of this the Lord certainly was not absent. When the Lamanites were put upon reservations, He was there. It was thought at first that the lands thus given were of little value to anyone and hence were good enough for the Indians.

However, the Lord had his hand in it all and was guiding these events. He was fully aware of His promises to the

Lamanites, and He was watching over them. He did three great things:

1. He brought His gospel to them. That was most important.

2. He put the Indians on reservation lands certain of which now have turned out to be rich in oil, uranium, gold, silver, and other metals, as well as coal, making some of the Indian tribes very wealthy.

3. He gave them self-government as fast as they were able to cope with it, and He provided schools to lift the red man and his children out of "obscurity and out of darkness." All this God did.

We must never suppose that the Lord forgets His promises. Every one will be fulfilled to the letter; not one "jot nor tittle" shall be lost. (Matthew 5:18.)

The Lamanites not only will be "carried on their shoulders" as the Gentiles begin to wait upon them, but they will enjoy the richest blessings of the gospel as they join the Church and assume the responsibility of such membership. Much has been done by the nations, and much must yet be done. Many of the Lamanites still suffer serious privations.

Including those in Alaska, in United States areas there is a total of 267 reservations for Indians, Aleuts, and Eskimos.

The total land area under the trusteeship of the United States Bureau of Indian Affairs is 51,789,251 acres.

Although some Indians, both in the west and in Oklahoma, have inherited rich rewards in oil wells and mining operations, the average per capita income of Indians living on federal reservations is estimated at only $1,500 a year. In urban areas the figure is $2,108 per capita, and in rural areas $1,142.

The 1976 birth rate was 30.7 live births for each 1,000 United States Indians and Alaska natives. The birth rate for all races in the nation was 14.8. The life expectancy at birth was 65.1 years compared to 70.9 for all races.

The infant death rate for Indians and Alaska natives in 1976 was 19.1 for every 1,000 live births, compared to the national overall rate of 15.2. In 1955, however, the infant death rate for Indians and Alaska natives was 62.5, compared to a national figure of 26.4. This remarkable improvement came as medicine and education were made more available.

Accidents were the leading cause of death among Indians and Alaska natives, with a rate of 159.2 per 100,000 population in 1976. Next came diseases of the heart, which caused 146.7 deaths; malignant neoplasms resulted in 83.8, and cirrhosis of the liver, 68.3.

The suicide rate in 1976 was 26 per 100,000 of population, compared to 12.6 for all races in America, twice as high as for the general population.

Many Indians live in good houses, with improved sanitary conditions, and are comparatively well off. Income from their mineral and oil products generally is concentrated under tribal care and is not given directly to individuals. Hence there are many Indians who live in sub-standard conditions even now.

Government figures for 1978 indicated that for 154,700 Indian families, there were only 126,675 housing units. A mere 64,500 of them were in standard condition, while 62,175 were below standard.

Only about 30,000 of these housing units were even worth renovating, according to the Indian Bureau itself.

Living conditions are reflected also in these figures:

The 1977 rate of new cases of tuberculosis per 100,000 of population for Indians and Alaska natives was 4.5 times as high as the rate among all races in the U.S.A. The age-adjusted 1976 death rate from tuberculosis was 9.5 times as great among the Indians and Alaska natives as among the general population.

It is estimated by the census bureau that among the American Indians there are presently 254,100 children under 16 years of age, while there are 356,700 persons between 16 and 65.

The number over 65 is uncertain, but one figure issued by the Indian Bureau is set at 38,000.

Although many advantages are offered to the Indians by the government, the results are spotty. Some on certain reservations prosper, while others who live elsewhere do not. An education is available in some districts, in others that opportunity is lacking.

The sale of liquor to the Indians is probably the greatest curse and the worst drawback facing them. Many who had been financially fairly well off disposed of their holdings for a fraction of their worth while under the influence of liquor.

Liquor seriously undermines their health and is also a major factor in accidents, which cause more deaths among the Indians than does any disease.

INDIAN
GOVERNMENT

CHAPTER THIRTEEN

When the Indians fought to preserve their lands and homes as the westward emigration continued, they were nearly always in a losing situation.

Superior numbers and better weapons gave a great advantage to their "paleface" intruders. Eventually they lost on all fronts and were confined to reservations, as is well known.

During this period the Indian affairs of the United States were securely in the hands of the War Department because the Indians were considered enemies of the country to be subdued through force of arms.

Once the Indians were confined to reservations, the government at Washington began to change its mind and perceived that those people deserved better treatment.

The Department of the Interior was given the responsibility of looking after them. Then the Bureau of Indian Affairs was established. Step by step, the "Great White Father" moved toward self-government for the Indians, and in cases where any had left the reservations, becoming more or less integrated into the general population, plans were made to give them full citizenship.

Government schools were provided and technical and professional help was given in the development of lands and industries.

Thirty percent of all the natural resources of the United States were found to be on Indian lands, with the Indian population being less than one half of one percent of the nation.

It was the hope of the Washington officials to elevate the Indian to the point where as many as possible would receive training in the professions, in various technical types of employment, and in improved agriculture.

Presently 95 percent of the Indian children between the ages of seven and thirteen are in school. Approximately twenty thousand young men and women are enrolled in college.

The general enlightenment stimulated the Indians' desire for self-government and, on an individual basis, self-determination.

It was decided in Washington to give the Indians a form of constitutional government on their own reservations. Tribal constitutions were written, legislative bodies were elected by the people. The central government was administered through a tribal council headed by a chairman and a vice-chairman.

When constitutional government was given to the Indians, their units were recognized as distinct political communities with basic domestic and municipal functions.

The tribe was empowered to define conditions of tribal membership, regulate domestic relations between members, prescribe rules of inheritance, levy taxes, provide legislative rules, administer justice, and provide punishment for violation of the laws on the reservation.

With the large number of Indians now being well educated, many of them in the professions and technical skills, they also have become very vocal in expressing their views.

This has led to the establishment of their own newspapers, magazines, and bulletins in various parts of the nation.

Oklahoma, once the refuge of a smitten people at the end of their "Trail of Tears," has become a national memorial to the red man.

The Indian Hall of Fame is there, in which Indian heroes and heroines of the past are presented in a rare display of bronze statuary. It is located at Anadarko.

Thirty-five tribes now inhabit the state of Oklahoma. Descendants of the original sixty-seven tribes inhabiting Indian Territory still live in Oklahoma, but some do not total a sufficient number to make up a tribe.

WHAT
BYU DOES

The Brigham Young University, at Provo, Utah, has what is probably the most outstanding program for the advancement of the Indians anywhere in the world.

Each year between six hundred and seven hundred Indian students seek degrees at that university. A bachelor's, master's or doctor's degree is offered to them in law, business, pre-med, general science, education, music, art, nursing, physical education, economics, political science, sociology, history, health, social work, law enforcement, public administration, counseling, engineering, languages, psychology, and other fields.

In 1980 there were seventy-four different Indian tribes represented in the enrollment. On that campus they have a yearly all-campus Indian Week celebration, they have a famous all-Indian choir, and they publish an Indian newspaper, "The Eagle's Eye." They have an all-Indian campus club known as the Tribe of Many Feathers. The university offers a fully certified Indian Studies minor.

The orientation of the Indian Education Program at BYU is to increase its efforts to educate the student rather than to lower the academic requirements. The department assumes that the Indian student can learn as well as any other student and that the academic disadvantages of some Indian students can be overcome with increased effort on the part of the student and of the faculty and other supporting elements of the educational process.

The Indian Education Department believes in self-determination and expects every student to work hard and to do his or her best to achieve excellence in academic performance. The requirements for graduation of Indian students are the same as those for other students.

The students perform well in the traditional classroom, but they gain their most effective training by working productively in campus, community, and reservation projects which improve the quality of their people's lives.

They tutor Indian youth in grade and high schools. They serve as student teachers and counselors in school districts with large Indian enrollments.

In such districts they help train faculty to teach Indian students effectively, and they consult with parents and faculty in solving individual problems.

Their original plays and music, their inter-tribal choir, and their performing group, "The Lamanite Generation," represent a renaissance in traditional Indian culture.

They serve throughout the world as emissaries of the Indian people and offer the most hope-instilling examples of creativity, poise, and self-esteem that many Indian young people ever see.

One of the most practical helps offered the Indian students at Brigham Young University comes through the American Indian Services and Research Center (AISRC) at the university.

It has been in operation since 1958. It conducts eighty-three on-going programs which are being implemented successfully on forty-one reservations.

AISRC started a trial "home gardening project" in the spring of 1976 with fifteen young Indian families. Various fruits and vegetables were planted and canned under the supervision and support of the AISRC. The program was an overwhelming success as these young couples were taught the fundamentals of planting and caring for a garden.

Hundreds of bushels of corn, tomatoes, squash, pumpkins, cherries and cantaloupes were harvested on a ten-acre plot.

Future plans call for establishing three other large garden plots for instructing additional young couples in home gardening.

Through the resources and support of the American Indian Services and Research Center, forty-five thousand tomato plants were transported and planted on twenty reservations located in the Southwest and along the Rio Grande. Hundreds of Indian families have participated in the two-year program. Already requests have been received from thirteen other Indian tribes to take part in the program.

Increased demands call for fifty thousand additional plants to be distributed in 1982.

A three-year fruit tree distribution program has provided over twelve thousand assorted peach, plum, pear, apricot, and cherry trees for American Indian families on thirty-five reservations.

THE
GOSPEL COMES

Truly the "morning breaks, the shadows flee" as the restored gospel is taken to the Lamanites. It is a glorious day. It is in fulfillment of the prophecies of old. This is a time of destiny. The Lamanites are returning to Christ.

President Spencer W. Kimball, long an advocate of the work among the Lamanites, expressed this exalted view:

"The Lamanites must rise in majesty and power. We must look forward to the day when they will be "white and delightsome" (2 Nephi 30:6), sharing the freedoms and blessings which we enjoy; when they shall have economic security, culture, refinement, and education; when they shall be operating farms and businesses and industries and shall be occupied in the professions and in teaching; when they shall be organized into wards and stakes of Zion, furnishing much of their own leadership; when they shall build and occupy and fill the temples, and serve in them as the natives are now serving in the Hawaiian Temple where I found last year the entire service conducted by them and done perfectly.

"And in the day when their prophet shall come, one shall rise . . . mighty among them . . . being an instrument in the hands of God, with exceeding faith, to work mighty wonders. . . . (2 Nephi 3:24.)

"Brothers and Sisters, the florescence of the Lamanites is in our hands." (CR, October 1947, p. 22.)

President Heber J. Grant spoke of it in this way:

"God gave us the Book of Mormon and the chief reason, as set forth in one of the revelations, is that it shall be the means of bringing to the descendants of Father Lehi the knowledge of the Redeemer of the world, and to establish them in the faith of their fathers.

"I bear witness to you that nothing on earth shall ever bring them out of their thraldom save the gospel of the Lord Jesus Christ. I rejoice, therefore, that the day dawn is breaking, the night is dispelling and the day of their redemption cometh." (CR, October 1926, p. 40.)

The fruition of these prophecies begins to appear in the entire western hemisphere and down through the Polynesian chain of islands.

It had a small beginning, with a few missionaries sent here, and a few more there, in the days of the Prophet Joseph, who envisioned the glorious project and looked to its ultimate fulfillment.

Conversions began on a small scale, too. Little branches were formed by the missionaries at first, then districts, and ultimately stakes, until now there are stakes throughout Mexico, Central America, and South America, and down through the well-populated islands of Polynesia.

And temples too—in Hawaii, New Zealand, Mexico City, and more in Tonga, Samoa, and Tahiti, serving the people of Lehi. What a remarkable thing—temples of their own for the people of Lehi! And in addition to those, there is the Arizona Temple at Mesa, which for years itself has been virtually a Lamanite temple and has served thousands of Lamanites from Panama to Phoenix and the Indian reservations thereabout. It will still give such service, augmenting the work to be done in Mexico City.

Eventually there will be a gathering of many Lamanites to Zion—Jackson County. There they will join with Ephraim, the birthright tribe in Israel, in not only helping to build the city of New Jerusalem but in erecting the mighty temple that is to be built in that city.

It was this great promise that inspired President Charles W. Penrose to write the following lines while he was still a missionary in England in 1855:

A "white, delightsome people" they shall be,
A fruitful branch of Israel's olive tree.
The promises old Father Jacob spake
Shall be fulfilled for holy Joseph's sake;
The mighty God of Jacob shall increase
Their strength and glory, numbers, wealth and peace;
From Heaven above and earth beneath shall flow
The richest blessings they can have below.
The holy royal priesthood they shall wield,
Eternal powers upon them shall be sealed.

The tribes of Israel shall be blest by them,
They'll help to build the New Jerusalem.
        (Copyright 1950, Ruth McQuarrie Penrose.)

There are numerous references to the fact that the believing Lamanites will assist Ephraim, or the Latter-day Saints, in building the New Jerusalem in Jackson County.

President Anthony W. Ivins, first counselor to President Heber J. Grant, said:

"These Lamanites are heirs to the promises, and God has said, without qualification, that he will give this land to them for an everlasting inheritance (3 Nephi 20:13-14); that they shall be, with us, the builders of the new Jerusalem (3 Nephi 21:20-25); the powers of heaven shall be among them, and they shall know the record of their fathers which has been brought to us through the instrumentality of the Prophet Joseph Smith." (CR, April 1915, p. 112.)

President Joseph Fielding Smith also explains that the Lamanites will assist Ephraim, who holds the birthright in Israel, in the construction of the New Jerusalem. He says:

"That the remnants of Joseph found among the descendants of Lehi will have part in this great work is certainly consistent, and the great work of this restoration, the building of the temple and the City of Zion or New Jerusalem, will fall to the lot of the descendants of Joseph, but it is Ephraim who will stand at the head and direct the work." (*Doctrines of Salvation*, compiled by Bruce R. McConkie, Vol. 2, p. 251.)

President Smith makes it clear that Ephraim, holding the birthright in Israel, always stands at the head of this latter-day work, but as part of the redemption of the Lamanites, wrought out through Ephraim, the descendants of Lehi will be permitted to assist in the great work in Jackson County.

President Wilford Woodruff taught: "Every word that God has ever said of them will have its fulfillment, and they, by and by, will receive the gospel.

"It will be a day of God's power among them, and a nation will be born in a day. Their chiefs will be filled with the power of God and receive the gospel, and they will go forth and help build the new Jerusalem." (JD 15:272.)

When the Savior visited this continent after His resurrection, He told the Nephites that if the Gentiles would repent and soften their hearts, the Church would be established among them, and they would have the privilege of joining with the Lamanites in the building of the New Jerusalem. (3 Nephi 21:22-24.)

61

"If they [the Gentiles] will repent and hearken unto my words and harden not their hearts, I will establish my Church among them and they shall come in unto the covenant and be numbered among this remnant of Jacob unto whom I have given this land for their inheritance.

"And they shall assist my people, the remnant of Jacob, and also as many of the house of Israel as shall come, that they may build a city which shall be called the New Jerusalem.

"And then shall they assist my people that they may be gathered upon all the face of the land in unto the New Jerusalem." (3 Nephi 21:22-24.)

Ephraim will assist them in the sense of bringing them the gospel and providing the ordinances of salvation. As President Smith says, Ephraim has the birthright or presidency position. Through Ephraim's ministry the Lamanites will be assisted, as are all other converts, and in turn they will assist Ephraim by their efforts and obedience, following their conversion.

Six hundred years before Christ the prophet Nephi said:

". . . And then shall they rejoice; for they shall know that it is a blessing unto them from the hand of God; and their scales of darkness shall begin to fall from their eyes; and many generations shall not pass away among them, save they shall be a white and delightsome people." (2 Nephi 30:6.)

Elder Orson Pratt of the Council of the Twelve in pioneer times said this very interesting thing concerning the redemption of the Lamanites:

"This people—the Latter-day Saints, before they can ever return to build up the waste places of Zion and receive their inheritances in Jackson County, Missouri, have got to exert themselves to bring the remnants of Joseph to a knowledge of the truth." (JD 17:299.)

THE GOSPEL TO
THE LAMANITES

Beneficial as have been the advantages given to the Lamanites by the American government, their greatest blessing came when the restored gospel was given to them.

It opened their eyes to their past, provided faith in the Lord, and showed them the divine plan for their future.

The advantages given them by the government provided education, business opportunities, and the possibility of integration into the main white population, but the gospel gave them admittance to the kingdom of God.

The prophecies of the Book of Mormon are now fulfilled, with the Lamanites receiving the saving ordinances on an equal basis with all others who come into the Church.

When the gospel was restored through the Prophet Joseph Smith, the Lord made it abundantly clear that the word of God must be taken to the descendants of Lehi.

The frontispiece of the Book of Mormon also revealed this, as did the various writings of the prophets. The frontispiece declared that the Book of Mormon was "written to the Lamanites, who are a remnant of the house of Israel." Thus the Lamanites were divinely identified as Israelites, as heirs to the sacred promises.

The book, according to this frontispiece, was "written and sealed up and hid up unto the Lord, that" it might not be destroyed. It was "to come forth by the gift and power of God" for both Jew and Gentile, "sealed by the hand of Moroni and hid up unto the Lord to come forth in due time by way of the Gentile."

It was decreed, therefore, that the Lamanites were to receive this record as part of the restored gospel—"by way of the Gentile."

The Prophet Joseph, therefore, felt a particular responsibility to take the gospel to "the Lamanites." As early as July of 1828 the Lord, by revelation, made it known that "this testimony shall come to the knowledge of the Lamanites and the Lemuelites and the Ishmaelites who dwindle in unbelief because of the iniquity of their fathers whom the Lord had suffered to destroy the Nephites because of their iniquities and their abominations.

"And for this very purpose are these plates preserved which contain these records, that the promises of the Lord might be fulfilled which he made to his people, and that the Lamanites might come to the knowledge of their fathers and that they might know the promises of the Lord and that they may believe the gospel and rely upon the merits of Jesus Christ and be glorified through faith in his name and that through their repentance they might be saved." (D&C 3:18-20.)

This was the design of the Lord. Now today's Lamanites, descendants of those ancient rebellious brothers, eventually may be glorified through the gospel of Christ.

An interesting comment was made by the Lord in his revelation of March 1830 when he said to Martin Harris: "I command thee that thou shalt not covet thine own property but impart it freely to the printing of the Book of Mormon which contains the truth and the word of God—which is my word to the Gentile that soon it may go to the Jew, *of whom the Lamanites are a remnant*, that they may have the gospel." (D&C 19:26-27. Italics added.)

There is no doubt from these scriptures that the Lamanites are of the house of Israel, and "a remnant of the Jews," referring of course to their former residence at and their departure from Jerusalem under the leadership of the prophet Lehi.

It is to be remembered that they are not of the tribe of Judah, except as the blood of Mulek and his group was mixed among them following Mulek's arrival in America. Lehi was of Manasseh and Ishmael was of Ephraim.

The prophet Joseph immediately began his preparations for missions to the Lamanites. As in other things, he led the way, and he personally took part in preaching the gospel to them.

By revelation Oliver Cowdery, closest associate of the Prophet Joseph, was called on a mission to the Lamanites. This revelation came in September 1830, just six months after the organization of the Church. It said:

"And now behold I say unto you, that thou shall go unto the Lamanites and preach my gospel unto them, and inasmuch as they receive thy teachings thou shalt cause my Church to be established among them." (D&C 28:8.)

This calling was reiterated by the Lord when Peter Whitmer, Jr., was appointed to go with Oliver:

"Behold, I say unto you, Peter, that you shall take your journey with your brother Oliver; for the time has come that it is expedient in me that you shall open your mouth to declare my gospel; therefore, fear not, but give heed unto the words and advice of your brother, which he shall give you.

"And be you afflicted in all his afflictions, ever lifting up your heart unto me in prayer and faith, for his and your deliverance; for I have given unto him power to build up my church among the Lamanites." (D&C 30:5-6.)

THE MISSION
BEGINS

Oliver Cowdery and Peter Whitmer, Jr., were called of the Lord to go west and preach the gospel to the Lamanites. Other brethren approached the Prophet with an interest in this mission, and as a result, Parley P. Pratt and Ziba Peterson were also appointed at the conference held September 26, 1830, in Fayette.

Ziba Peterson was one of the early converts to the restored gospel and was among the first baptized into the new Church. At the first conference of the Church he had been ordained an elder.

Parley P. Pratt had lived near Cleveland, Ohio, a preacher for the so-called "Disciples," or Campbellites, led by Alexander Campbell, living in the vicinity of Kirtland, Ohio. He first heard of the Book of Mormon while on a preaching tour for that sect. He was baptized by Elder Cowdery a short time later.

The four missionaries left on their journey in the fall of 1830. They first went to Buffalo, New York, where they visited the Catteraugus Indians, leaving two copies of the Book of Mormon with some of the Indians who could read.

They then proceeded to Kirtland to visit Elder Pratt's friends of the Campbellite faith. Sidney Rigdon lived near there.

Sidney joined the Church, with nearly two hundred others of his congregation. He continued to preach the restored gospel to them even after the missionaries left. A branch of the Church was organized there at that early time.

It was a profitable two weeks that the missionaries spent in the area of Kirtland. But they were called to go to the Lamanites and, therefore, resumed their journey westward.

Elder Parley P. Pratt described their hardships en route to Jackson County, Missouri, as follows:

"We traveled on foot for three hundred miles through vast prairies and through trackless wilds of snow — no beaten road; houses few and far between; and the bleak northwest wind always blowing in our faces with a keenness which would almost take the skin off the face.

"We traveled for whole days, from morning till night, without a house or fire, wading in snow to the knees at every step, and the cold so intense that the snow did not melt on the south side of the houses, even in the midday sun, for nearly six weeks.

"We carried on our backs our changes of clothing, several books, and corn bread and raw pork. We often ate our frozen bread and pork by the way, when the bread would be so frozen that we could not bite or penetrate any part of it but the outside crust." (*Autobiography of Parley P. Pratt*, Deseret Book Co., p. 52.)

They traversed fifteen hundred miles under such difficulties, arriving in Independence in January, 1831. They were four months on the trip, but during that time they had preached to two tribes of Indians, the Catteraugus in New York and the Wyandotts in Ohio.

In Missouri they now met with the chiefs of the Delaware tribe and were well received. Most of the Indians were unable to read, but the brethren left copies of the Book of Mormon with the few who could read.

One of the chiefs said:

" 'We feel truly thankful to our white friends who have come so far and been at such pains to tell us good news, and especially this news concerning the Book of our forefathers. It makes us glad in here' he added as he placed his hand over his heart." (Ibid. p. 56.)

It was not long, however, until the sectarian priests became aroused. They made complaints to the Indian agents in charge of the territory, after which the missionaries were forbidden further access to the Indian country.

With this turn of events, the brethren began work in

Jackson County, Missouri, among the white settlers. Since they had disposed of all copies of the Book of Mormon which they had brought with them, they decided that Parley P. Pratt should return to Kirtland to obtain more. This was in February, 1831.

The Prophet himself preached to the Indians on several occasions. Under date of August 12, 1841, he recorded:

"A considerable number of the Sac and Fox Indians have been for several days encamped in the neighborhood of Montrose. The ferrymen brought over a great number on the ferryboat and two flat boats for the purpose of visiting me.

"The military band and a detachment of Invincibles (part of the Legion) were on shore ready to receive and escort them to the grove, but they refused to come on shore until I went down. I accordingly went down, and met Keokuk, Kis-ku-kosh, Appenoose, and about one hundred chiefs and braves of those tribes, with their families.

"At the landing, I was introduced by Brother Hyrum to them; and after salutations, I conducted them to the meeting grounds in the grove, and instructed them in many things which the Lord had revealed unto me concerning their fathers, and the promises that were made concerning them in the Book of Mormon. I advised them to cease killing each other and warring with other tribes; also to keep peace with the whites; all of which was interpreted to them.

"Keokuk replied that he had a Book of Mormon at his wigwam which I had given him some years before. 'I believe,' said he, 'you are a great and good man; I look rough, but I also am a son of the Great Spirit. I have heard your advice—we intend to quit fighting, and follow the good talks you have given us.'

"After the conversation they were feasted on the green with good food, dainties, and melons by the brethren; and they entertained the spectators with a specimen of their dancing."

Early in July, 1843, the Prophet had an interview with several chiefs of the Pottawattamie tribe who had come to visit him in Nauvoo. A description of this event is given by Wilford Woodruff, as he recorded it in his journal:

"The Indian chiefs remained at Nauvoo until the Prophet returned and had his trial. During their stay they had a talk with Hyrum Smith in the basement of the Nauvoo House. Wilford Woodruff and some others were present. They were not free to talk, and did not wish to communicate their feelings until they could see the great Prophet.

"At length, on the 2nd day of July, 1843, President Joseph Smith and several of the Twelve met those chiefs in the court-room, with about twenty of the elders. The following is a synopsis of the conversation which took place as given by the interpreter: —

"The Indian orator arose and asked the Prophet if the men who were present were all his friends. Answer — 'Yes.'

"He then said — 'We as a people have long been distressed and oppressed. We have been driven from our lands many times. We have been wasted away by wars, until there are but few of us left. The white man has hated us and shed our blood, until it has appeared as though there would soon be no Indians left. We have talked with the Great Spirit, and the Great Spirit has talked with us. We have asked the Great Spirit to save us and let us live; and the Great Spirit has told us that he had raised up a great Prophet, chief, and friend, who would do us great good and tell us what to do; and the Great Spirit has told us that you are the man (pointing to the Prophet Joseph). We have now come a great way to see you, and hear your words, and to have you to tell us what to do. Our horses have become poor traveling, and we are hungry. We will now wait and hear your word.'

"The Spirit of God rested upon the Lamanites, especially the orator. Joseph was much affected and shed tears. He arose and said unto them: 'I have heard your words. They are true. The Great Spirit has told you the truth. I am your friend and brother, and I wish to do you good. Your fathers were once a great people. They worshiped the Great Spirit. The Great Spirit did them good. He was their friend; but they left the Great Spirit, and would not hear his words or keep them. The Great Spirit left them, and they began to kill one another, and they have been poor and afflicted until now.

"The Great Spirit has given me a book, and told me that you will soon be blessed again. The Great Spirit will soon begin to talk with you and your children. This is the book which your fathers made. I wrote upon it (showing them the Book of Mormon). This tells what you will have to do. I now want you to begin to pray to the Great Spirit. I want you to make peace with one another, and do not kill any more Indians: it is not good. Do not kill white men; it is not good; but ask the Great Spirit for what you want, and it will not be long before the Great Spirit will bless you, and you will cultivate the earth and build good houses like white men. We will give you something to eat and to take home with you.'

"When the Prophet's words were interpreted to the chiefs, they all said it was good. The chief asked, 'How many moons would it be before the Great Spirit would bless them?' He (Joseph) told them, Not a great many.

"At the close of the interview, Joseph had an ox killed for them, and they were furnished with some more horses, and they went home satisfied and contented." (DHC Vol. 5, p. 479.)

SOUTH SEAS
MISSIONS

The missions to the Polynesians in the South Seas, whom the Prophet felt were of the house of Lehi, became one of the great enterprises of the Church during the final years of Joseph Smith.

As early as 1843 he inaugurated this work, but as time progressed more elders were sent to the islands. The stature of the missionaries is evidenced by the fact that some of them subsequently became members of the Council of the Twelve and of the First Presidency.

President Lorenzo Snow and President Joseph F. Smith were among them, both of whom later presided over the Church.

When the Prophet Joseph was planning his work for the Lamanites, he had two groups of people in mind, the American Indians in the United States and the many natives on the Pacific Islands from Hawaii to New Zealand. He felt they were all of Lehi.

At a council meeting held in Nauvoo on May 23, 1843, the Prophet called Elder Addison Pratt to become a seventy and to accept a mission in the Pacific Islands. President Brigham Young ordained him a seventy and set him apart as a missionary, assisted by Elders Heber C. Kimball, Orson Hyde, and Parley P. Pratt. His call was to the Society Islands, of which Tahiti is the largest island.

Three other brethren were called at the same time, Elders Noah Rogers, Benjamin Grouard and Knowlton F. Hanks. They were to go to the islands with Addison Pratt.

In his blessing President Young said to Elder Pratt: "We commit the keys of the opening the gospel to the Society Islands to you."

Before leaving for his mission, Elder Pratt presented a whale's tooth, the tooth of a South Sea seal, some coral, the bones of the wing of an albatross and the jaw-bone of a porpoise for a beginning of the Nauvoo museum.

The brethren went to New Bedford to board ship, and left on the S.S. *Timoleon* on October 9, 1833. While still at sea, Elder Hanks died. After having traveled around the Horn, the other three brethren landed in the Society Islands in May, 1844, and in July following, a branch had been established amongst the Polynesian people.

Missionaries were sent to Hawaii and New Zealand, as well as to Samoa, Tahiti, and Tonga in those early days.

The gospel was readily accepted by the natives when they learned the significance of the Book of Mormon to them.

Two of the great mission presidents to serve in New Zealand became General Authorities, Elder Rufus K. Hardy, later of the First Council of the Seventy, and Elder Matthew Cowley, who in 1945 became a member of the Council of the Twelve Apostles.

Elder Hardy deeply believed that all of the Polynesians were related, regardless of which islands they lived on. He was able to be understood wherever he went when he spoke Maori, and he wrote about it in Tahiti as follows:

"On this island, as well as on all other islands of the Tuamotu Group, I had demonstrated again and again the fact that the language of these people, and the Maori people in New Zealand, and in many instances the languages of Tonga, are akin and that I could readily understand and be understood when speaking. In fact the people were eager to converse with me, and shed tears of joy at hearing what to them was their ancient and sacred language. . . .

"And I am astounded at the persistence of the one language which runs eastward from New Zealand to Easter Island. An old gentleman told me that three hundred and thirty-five years ago his forefathers came from Easter Island — 'Rapanui,' and that only a few of the people remained there to take charge of the stone monoliths which had been hewn from the living rock.

"And when I told him about Kaitangata his face beamed, and he said, 'I marvel at your knowing about my ancestors.' When I told him it was not only his ancestors, but the common ancestor of the Maori people, of the Tongan and of the Samoan peoples, he was thrilled indeed. As we spoke to this people they were wiping tears from their eyes." (*Deseret News*, August 5, 1939, pp. 3 and 8.)

THE HAWAIIAN
MISSION

The Hawaiian Mission had its birth on December 12, 1850, when ten missionaries stepped off the sailing ship *The Imaum of Muscat* in Honolulu harbor.

Those missionaries were George Q. Cannon, James Keeler, William Farrer, Hiram Clark, Thomas Morris, Hiram Blackwell, James Hawkins, Thomas Whittle, Henry W. Bigler, and John Dixon.

The next day they ascended a mountain near Honolulu and dedicated the islands for the preaching of the gospel. Then they separated, with two elders being assigned to each of the larger islands.

The work grew rapidly. Several branches of the Church were organized on Maui during the first year of their labors and 196 were baptized.

By 1854 there were four thousand members on the various islands. Elder Cannon began translating the Book of Mormon in January of 1852, and the book was printed in California in 1855.

The missionaries were called back to Utah in 1858 due to the Johnston Army episode. Missionaries returned later and continued their work. Now at Laie are the temple and the Hawaii branch of BYU, and stakes cover the islands.

One of the outstanding missionaries to Hawaii in early days was Elder Joseph F. Smith, who later became President of the Church. When he was but fifteen years of age he was called on this mission and was set apart by Elder Parley P. Pratt of the Council of the Twelve.

A group of twenty-one missionaries received calls to go to the Pacific Islands at the April conference of the Church in 1854.

Hardly had Elder Smith arrived there than he became ill and suffered for weeks with a high fever. However, he filled a remarkable mission, becoming one of the presiding elders there by the time he was sixteen. He was highly adept at the native language.

Returning to Utah at the time of the Johnston Army affair, he served there until called on a mission to Great Britain, and then a second time to Hawaii.

Elder Ezra T. Benson and Elder Lorenzo Snow of the Council of Twelve went there also and Joseph F. Smith accompanied them. As they neared the islands on this trip, one of the miraculous events of the mission took place. It is described by President Joseph Fielding Smith, also a subsequent president of the Church, and son of Elder Joseph F. Smith.

In the *Life of Joseph F. Smith*, by Joseph Fielding Smith (Deseret Book Company, p. 212-216), we read:

"They came to anchor one mile from the little harbor of Lahaina. At the time the sea was rough and the captain made ready to land his passengers in the ship's freight boat, which was unwieldy and not easily managed, especially in a rough sea. A breakwater had been constructed at the harbor, and by it the natives were protected when they ran their boats ashore. However, in approaching it, there was always danger of disaster and great skill was required, for at this point two seas met as described by Paul in his shipwreck off the coast of Melita.

"Joseph F. Smith who had traveled back and forth between the islands of Maui and Lanai many times on his first mission, realized the danger and tried to persuade the captain of the ship and Elders Benson and Snow, not to land at that particular time under the circumstances confronting them.

"He plead earnestly with them, but he was a young man, and the brethren felt it was his place to take counsel, not to give it; moreover, being unacquainted with the nature of the sea at this place, they did not feel the anxiety which the younger man felt.

"Following the suggestion of the captain, Elders Benson and Snow of the Council of the Apostles and their two companions, Elder Alma L. Smith and William W. Cluff, entered the boat and started for shore. Joseph F. Smith stoutly refused to go, leaving a feeling in the minds of his brethren that he was disobedient to counsel.

74

"In his endeavor to persuade these brethren not to go, Joseph F. volunteered to make the journey alone and bring back a better boat, but they were determined in their course. At his earnest request they did, however, leave their baggage on the ship in his care but this they did reluctantly.

"Besides the four brethren, the boat contained some boxes and barrels, the captain, two or three native passengers, and the boat's crew, who were natives. As the boat neared the shore Joseph F. watched in great anxiety and prayed earnestly that they might land in safety. When the boat left the ship the brethren thought his fears were ungrounded. Elder William W. Cluff describing the incident has said:

" 'The entrance to the harbor is a very narrow passage between coral reefs, and when the sea is rough, it is very dangerous, on account of the breakers. Where the vessel lay, the sea was not rough, but only presented the appearance of heavy swells rolling to the shore.

" 'As we approached the reef it was evident to me that the surf was running higher than we anticipated. I called the captain's attention to the fact. We were running quartering across the waves, and I suggested that we change our course so as to run at right angles with them. He replied that he did not think there was any danger, and our course was not changed.

" 'We went but a little further, when a heavy swell struck the boat and carried us before it about fifty yards. When the swell passed it left us in a trough between two huge waves. It was too late to retrieve our error, and we must run our chances. When the second swell struck the boat, it raised the stern so high that the steerman's oar was out of the water, and he lost control of the boat. It rode on the swell a short distance and swung around just as the wave began to break up. We were almost instantly capsized into the dashing, foaming sea.

" 'I felt no concern for myself about drowning, for while on my former mission I had learned to swim and sport in the surf of those shores. The last I remember of Brother Snow, was as the boat was going over. I saw him seize the upper edge of it with both hands; fearing that the upper edge of the boat or the barrels might hit and injure me as the boat was going over, I plunged head foremost into the water. After swimming a short distance, I came to the surface without being strangled or injured.

" 'The boat was bottom upwards, and barrels, hats and umbrellas were floating in every direction, I swam to the boat and as there was nothing to cling to on the bottom, I reached under and seized the edge of it. About the same time Brother Benson came up near me and readily got hold of the boat.

" 'Brother Alma L. Smith came up on the opposite side of the boat from Brother Benson and myself. He was considerably strangled, but succeeded in securing a hold on the boat. A short time afterwards the captain was discovered, about fifty yards from us. Two sailors, one on each side of him, succeeded in keeping him on the surface.

" 'Although he was able to swim he was holding in his hands a sack of $400 or $500 silver dollars which imperiled his life, but notwithstanding that he refused to let go and under those conditions was rescued.

" 'Nothing yet had been seen of Brother Snow, although the natives had been swimming and diving in every direction in search of him. We were only about one-fourth of a mile from shore.'

"The people on shore sensing the danger as the boat approached the shore manned a life boat and hurried to the scene and assisted the drenched passengers and crew to their boat. Accomplishing this the crew wanted to row for the shore, and pick up the captain on their way. Elder Cluff suggested that a second boat that had put off from the shore was nearer the captain and would pick him up and that one other passenger was still missing, so the crew of the first boat consented to remain and make further search.

"Finally one of the natives in edging himself around the capsized boat, felt Brother Snow with his feet and turned and pulled him out from under the boat. His body was stiff and apparently life was gone. There was little doubt in the minds of any of those present that he was dead.

"His devoted brethren laid his body across their knees and with faith prayed over him while the natives declared there was no use. At last the brethren endeavored to stimulate breathing by compressing his chest and breathing in his mouth and drawing the air out again. It was one hour or more after the accident when the first signs of life returned. When he had recovered sufficiently he was taken to the home of a Portuguese who kindly proffered his hospitality.

"Brother Snow when he had recovered stated that as

76

they were moving along about half the distance between the boat and the shore, his attention was suddenly arrested by Captain Fisher calling to the oarsmen, in a voice which denoted some alarm, 'Hurry up, hurry up!'

" 'I quickly discovered the cause of the alarm,' said Brother Snow. 'A short distance behind us, I saw an immense surf, rushing towards us swifter than a race horse. We had scarcely a moment for reflection before the huge mass was upon us. In an instant our boat, with its contents, as though it were only a feather, was hurled into the briny water, and we were under this rolling, seething, mountain wave.'

"It came so rapidly that it apparently took all in the boat by surprise. Elder Snow, it seems, was thrown under the boat where he remained for a great length of time while all the rest of the passengers and crew were being rescued from the briny water. How long he was there nobody knows for in the excitement there was no thought of measuring the time, but to all it seemed part of eternity. It was sufficiently long, however, as the incidents of the occasion can testify, for a man in similar condition to be completely drowned.

"It is very evident if the Lord had not come to the rescue through the faith and administration of the Elders that Elder Lorenzo Snow would not have recovered, notwithstanding the manipulations resorted to. The brethren prayed and administered to him and worked over him, having him across their knees on the way to the shore, a distance of nearly half a mile.

"When they reached the shore they carried him to some empty barrels on the sandy beach, laid him face downward on a barrel and rolled him back and forth and by this means they got much of the water he had swallowed out of him. Then resorting to artificial breathing, and placing mouth to mouth and blowing down his throat and then sucking the air back again, eventually they discovered signs of life returning. This must have been one full hour after the upsetting of the boat.

"While all of this was going on, Elder Joseph F. Smith stood on the ship watching intensely and in great anxiety all that was taking place, but helpless to assist his stricken brethren except by his faith and prayers. He could see that some one was in dire distress but from his point of view could not tell the extent of the injury or who it was that was stricken.

"It was a great relief to him when later he was able

to gain the shore and meet his brethren who had refused to accept his earnest pleading and looked upon him as a stubborn young man who should have accepted the decision of his brethren.

"President Snow declared that after this incident the Lord revealed to him that this young man, Joseph F. Smith, who had refused to get off the vessel that had carried them from San Francisco to Honolulu, and then to the harbor of Lahaina, and get in the whale-boat to go to shore, would some day be the Prophet of God on the earth."

George Q. Cannon was one of the great missionaries to the Polynesians. He went to Hawaii when he was but 23 years of age. He arrived in Honolulu in December of 1850 with the other elders so assigned.

Amid discouraging circumstances, Elder Cannon proceeded to work among the native Hawaiians, and within six weeks after his arrival he was organizing branches of the Church.

His acquiring of the native language was attributed by him to a miraculous power. Elder Cannon, with the assistance of four other elders, in three-and-one-half years added to the Church over four thousand souls.

In 1855 President George Q. Cannon, having translated the Book of Mormon into the Hawaiian language, together with his companions, Joseph Bull and Matthew F. Wilkie, had printed an edition of 2,000 copies.

PRESIDENTS
SMITH AND McKAY

Presidents George Albert Smith and David O. McKay were two other laborers in the Polynesian Islands who became presidents of the Church.

President Smith accompanied Elder Rufus K. Hardy on tours throughout the South Sea area. President McKay visited there earlier when making his world tour of all the missions of the Church.

President McKay experienced some unusual spiritual events on that tour, one of note in Samoa. These occurrences included the miraculous gift of tongues. His tour took place in 1921.

President McKay was accompanied on this journey by President Hugh J. Cannon of Liberty Stake, who was appointed to this responsibility by the First Presidency. A monument now stands in Samoa to the memory of President McKay, and the Saints there annually celebrate his coming.

President Smith and Elder Hardy made their tour in 1938.

They first went to Hawaii and visited the two missions then headquartered there, the Hawaiian Mission and the Japanese Mission.

On February 7 of that year they sailed for Sidney and Melbourne, Australia. From there in March they went to Auckland, New Zealand, thence going to the Tongan Mission.

Following that visit the two travelers sailed to New Zealand in April to take part in a conference there. Then they returned to Samoa to participate in the annual "David O. McKay Day."

Before they left Salt Lake City on this journey, a public reception was held in their honor, again exhibiting the high interest of Church members in the work in Polynesia.

Of this reception the *Deseret News* wrote on January 10, 1938:

"At the public reception for George Albert Smith and Rufus K. Hardy—who on February 1st next will leave to forward the interests of the Church in the Hawaiian Islands, Samoa, Tahiti, New Zealand and Australia—friends of the two outstanding churchmen paid their respects to them in a series of eulogies which must have been highly gratifying and inspiring to them.

"Among the speakers who hailed the leadership of Honorable George Albert Smith in commemorating Utah history were Heber J. Grant, L. D. S. Church president; William M. Jeffers, president of the Union Pacific Railroad; and members of the Pioneer Trails and Landmarks' Association, whose executive committee sponsored the testimonial gathering.

"Among other spontaneous yet endearing testimonies to the worth and work of these twain prospective voyagers, President Grant said of George Albert Smith that he is one of the most energetic, splendid, hard-working men in the Council of the Twelve Apostles; and Mr. Jeffers called for a return to the pioneer way of thinking."

MATTHEW COWLEY'S SAGA

The name of Matthew Cowley is legend in New Zealand but also in the other islands where the Polynesians live.

Although many missionaries preceded him to New Zealand, including Elder Rufus K. Hardy, who served there with great distinction, there is a special aura about the labors of Elder Cowley.

He spent thirteen years among the native population of New Zealand. He preached the gospel, performed miracles, particularly of healing, translated the Book of Mormon, and was considered one of the dearest friends of the natives.

They called him Matiu Kauri, which is Maori for "giant tree." When he lived among them he drew the natives to him like a magnet. When he died he was mourned from one end of the island chain to the other.

Many called him tumuaki, a term of endearment, which also means president. He presided over the mission for years, and still later, as the Apostle of the Lord in charge of all the Pacific Islands, he labored for an extended period.

When he received his patriarchal blessing as a child of six, the patriarch, Elder Luther C. Burnham of Mancos, Colorado, said:

"Thou shalt live to be a mighty man in Israel, for thou art of royal seed, the seed of Jacob through Joseph.

"Thou shalt become a great and mighty man in the eyes of the Lord and become an ambassador of Christ to the uttermost bounds of the earth. Your understanding shall become great and your wisdom reach to heaven. . . . The Lord will give you the mighty faith of the brother of Jared, for thou shalt know that He lives and that the gospel of

Jesus Christ is true, even in your youth." (*Matthew Cowley, Man of God*, Smith, Bookcraft, p. 4.)

Matthew was called on his island mission when but seventeen years old. He struggled for weeks over the language and finally received it by the gift of tongues.

Soon after his arrival there he was left without a companion for three months, but he carried on his ministry with the aid of the faithful Saints among whom he lived.

He told often of the faith of the Maoris. For example, he was approached by a native woman who asked him to come to her home, her son having been injured in a fall from a tree. "My boy is hurt. You fix him up," she said.

The young elder administered to the child, who was lying prone on the floor of her home, and as soon as the elder had finished his blessing the boy went out and began climbing trees again.

A branch president had been ill for a week with a high fever. Elder Cowley was sent for. He blessed the man, who was made well immediately. He blessed sterile couples and they were able to have children.

A woman had elephantitis. She said, "Brother Cowley, bless me and remove from me this dread disease." He did, and she was made well.

A native father brought a child to be named by Elder Cowley, and said, "While you are giving it a name, please give it its sight. It was born blind."

He gave the child its name, and blessed it for its vision, and the child was healed.

He told of a pearl diver who separated the pearls and put all the best in one pile. They were God's pearls, the diver said, and with these he paid his tithing.

A woman he had not seen before came to greet him in the village. He attempted to shake hands with her, but she refused, asking him to wait a short time. She went to her garden, dug into a hiding place, brought out a hundred dollars, and gave it to the elder. "This is my tithing," she said. "Now I can shake hands with the priesthood." (*Matthew Cowley Speaks*, p. 5-7, Deseret Book Company.)

So it was with Elder Cowley. Wherever he went he made friends among the Polynesians. Wherever he went he was a witness to their simple, child-like faith.

They were of the blood of Israel. They truly believed when they heard the gospel.

Today in New Zealand there are stakes and wards, missions and branches, schools of high rating, and a beautiful temple where the natives now work for both the living and the dead.

Prophecies continue to be fulfilled among them.

THE WORK
INCREASES

The missionary endeavor among the Lamanites has been eminently successful. These people are approaching a total of nearly three quarters of a million members.

There are missions to the Indian tribes of both the United States and Canada. Wherever we have a full-time mission in those nations, near which there are Indian tribes, the mission is assigned to take the gospel to them.

A great work has been done among the Navajos and the Hopis of the great Southwest. In that area we have all-Indian wards and all-Indian bishoprics. There are stake presidents and bishops of Lamanitish blood elsewhere also and they do well.

There are missions and stakes throughout the Polynesian Islands, as there are in Mexico and Central America. In the latter two countries there are about 250,000 members with the blood of Lehi in their veins. All are not of Manasseh; some are of Ephraim. Their blood has been mixed over the years. But they are of Israel.

There are missions with many members having the blood of Lehi in the South American countries.

One of the most successful undertakings of the Church among the Lamanites is the Indian Student Placement program. Each year as many as a thousand Indian children who are Church members are received from the United States reservations and taken into sponsors' homes for the school year.

With the permission of the Indian child's natural parents, the child is taken to a nearby area where there are good schools.

The child is taken into the home of a good Latter-day Saint family where he or she is treated on an equal basis with the other children.

Without any cost to the Indian child or his parents, the sponsor family virtually makes the child one with them for the duration of the school year.

He is housed, clothed, and fed along with the other children. He is taken to the city schools along with the other children, where he is given an education exactly like theirs.

At Christmas time, he may return to the reservation for a visit with his parents, then return to his foster home for the remainder of the school year, after which he again goes back to his home on the reservation.

A number of Indian children given this assistance have not only received a good elementary education but they have attended high school also. Many go on to college.

No evidence of racial prejudices appears in this program. Each child is given equal treatment.

The Indian tribal council members on the reservations have cooperated with this program, recognizing it as a means of providing a good education for children who may not have access to government schools on the reservation. There is no effort made to take the children out of the government schools. If they are able to attend there, that is where they go.

The Indian young people become skilled at various occupations and are trained in their own Church activities as well. A number of the young men are called on missions and serve successfully.

In Tonga and Samoa, particularly, but also in Tahiti, a large percentage of the LDS young people are educated in LDS schools and then go on missions, both boys and girls. They not only serve in their own home country but also are called to other lands, giving them a wider view of the world about them, even helping them to learn other languages where advisable.

The Church has provided day school in established educational systems in Mexico, Tonga, Tahiti, Samoa, Chile, and other places, where children not having access to the regular public schools of their country may receive an accredited education.

Hawaii has a branch of the Brigham Young University, provided especially for the South Sea native young people. They, too, are of Lehi, and the schools are a blessing to them.

Great opportunities for education are provided the Lamanites at the Brigham Young University in Provo, where hundreds attend each year, many of them obtaining degrees which of course help to assist them in earning a living.

Some who obtain business or nursing degrees, or certificates in teaching, return to the reservations to help their own people.

The day of the Lamanite indeed is here. The prophecies are being fulfilled. The Lamanites truly are beginning to blossom as the rose. Their future is bright. They will be among the choice children of God to meet the Savior when He comes.

CHURCH
OPPORTUNITIES

Men and boys of the blood of Lehi are given all the advantages of the priesthood of God equal to any and all other worthy male members of the Church.

The boys from twelve to eighteen are organized under the Aaronic Priesthood quorums; they are given religious duties to perform and are taught the gospel principles. From their own numbers presidencies of the quorums are appointed to direct their affairs.

Where the Boy Scout program is available, Indian boys become troop members and receive the same training as is given to all other boys of the same age.

Above the age of eighteen, worthy male members are given the Melchizedek Priesthood, as is the case with men of all racial groups. There is no distinction. The priesthood is a great leveler, all holders are brethren in the true sense of the word.

They, too, are organized into quorums, elders, seventies, and high priests, with particular duties assigned to each group. Many, especially of the younger men, are called on missions to preach to their own people, while some are sent to other lands, declaring the truths of the everlasting gospel.

Men and women alike are taught the importance of good family life which is the basis of our entire civilization and is established in our Church doctrines.

Every opportunity is given to faithful members of Lamanite descent that is provided for any and all others in the Church.

The Church-wide women's organization of the Relief Society has played an important role in the elevation of family life among the people of Lamanite blood.

Wherever the Church is organized into a branch or a ward, a Relief Society is formed as one of the basic units of the work.

All women are invited to join, and are taught sanitation, homemaking skills, care of infants, care of new mothers, diet and proper preparation of foods, needlework, and many other skills so important in any good home.

As an evidence of their contribution to the work of the Lamanites, it is now significant that in the South Pacific and the Far East there are approximately seventy-five thousand women who belong to the Relief Society, and in Mexico and South America there are another hundred thousand members.

The Relief Society assists women of all lands and all tongues as they come into the Church, uplifting their standard of living, intellectually, spiritually, and physically.

The aid the Relief Society has extended to the refugees from Asia, including the Cambodians and the Vietnamese, has been outstanding. But it does the same for the women of Britain, of all Europe, South Africa, and wherever the Church is established through the missionary system.

In this way, too, the gospel brings light to everyone who accepts it. Relief Society work is taught in 4,222 non-English-speaking wards and branches and in 8,650 where English is spoken.

The Primary organization for children under twelve is provided for all branches and wards of the Church regardless of geography or race or color.

The same is true of the Young Men's and Young Women's organizations for youth in the teenages. The program for these groups are athletic, cultural, and religious. It is the hope that each young person will grow up to be a faithful servant of Christ and a good citizen of the country in which he or she lives.

There are about 750,000 Lamanite members of the Church at this writing. They participate in both stake and missionary activities in Canada, the United States, Polynesia, Mexico, and Central America.

There are stakes and missions in ten South American countries, the people carrying on the work of the Church under their own local leadership. Most of the members in

South America can trace their ancestry as descendants of Lehi.

In the Polynesian Islands, about 90 percent of the total Church membership have similar lineage.

As the Church membership among the Lamanites continues toward the million mark, it becomes fully evident that the prophecies are fast being fulfilled.

Through these converts of today truly the family of Laman and Lemuel is flocking to the fold of their Redeemer, the Lord Jesus Christ.

Yes, the return of Laman and Lemuel is indeed a great modern miracle.